REA's Test Prep Books Are The Best!

(a sample of the <u>hundreds of letters</u> REA receives each year)

" CLEP success! I have bought and studied numerous CLEP guides, and this one has been the best! I was a bit rusty, being out of school for four years, but the [REA] guide . . . helped me get a perfect score! "

CLEP College Algebra Test-Taker, Guam

" My students report your chapters of review as the most valuable single resource they used for review and preparation. "

Teacher, American Fork, UT

" Your book was such a better value and was so much more complete than anything your competition has produced — and I have them all! "

Teacher, Virginia Beach, VA

" Compared to the other books that my fellow students had, your book was the most useful in helping me get a great score. "

Student, North Hollywood, CA

" Your book was responsible for my success on the exam, which helped me get into the college of my choice... I will look for REA the next time I need help. "

Student, Chesterfield, MO

" Just a short note to say thanks for the great support your book gave me in helping me pass the test... I'm on my way to a B.S. degree because of you! "

Student, Orlando, FL

(more on next page)

" I just wanted to thank you for helping me get a great score
on the AP U.S. History exam... Thank you for making great test preps! "
Student, Los Angeles, CA

" Your *Fundamentals of Engineering Exam* book was the absolute best
preparation I could have had for the exam, and it is one of the major
reasons I did so well and passed the FE on my first try. "
Student, Sweetwater, TN

" I used your book to prepare for the test and found that the advice and the
sample tests were highly relevant... Without using any other material, I earned
very high scores and will be going to the graduate school of my choice. "
Student, New Orleans, LA

" What I found in your book was a wealth of information sufficient to shore up
my basic skills in math and verbal... The section on analytical ability was
excellent. The practice tests were challenging and the answer explanations most
helpful. It certainly is the *Best Test Prep for the GRE*! "
Student, Pullman, WA

" I really appreciate the help from your excellent book. Please keep up
the great work. "
Student, Albuquerque, NM

" I am writing to thank you for your test preparation... your book helped me
immeasurably and I have nothing but praise for your *GRE* preparation."
Student, Benton Harbor, MI

(more on back page)

THE BEST TEST PREPARATION FOR THE

CLEP

COLLEGE-LEVEL EXAMINATION PROGRAM

COLLEGE ALGEBRA

Staff of Research & Education Association

Research & Education Association
61 Ethel Road West
Piscataway, New Jersey 08854

**The Best Test Preparation for the
CLEP COLLEGE ALGEBRA**

Year 2005 Printing

Copyright © 2004, 2001, 2000, 1998, 1996 by
Research & Education Association, Inc. All
rights reserved. No part of this book may be
reproduced in any form without permission of
the publisher.

Printed in the United States of America

Library of Congress Control Number 2003104648

International Standard Book Number 0-87891-898-1

REA® is a registered trademark of Research & Education Association, Inc.
Piscataway, New Jersey 08854.

ABOUT RESEARCH & EDUCATION ASSOCIATION

Founded in 1959, Research & Education Association is dedicated to publishing the finest and most effective educational materials—including software, study guides, and test preps—for students in middle school, high school, college, graduate school, and beyond.

REA's test preparation series includes books and software for all academic levels in almost all disciplines. Research & Education Association publishes test preps for students who have not yet completed high school, as well as high school students preparing to enter college. Students from countries around the world seeking to attend college in the United States will find the assistance they need in REA's publications. For college students seeking advanced degrees, REA publishes test preps for many major graduate school admission examinations in a wide variety of disciplines, including engineering, law, and medicine. Students at every level, in every field, with every ambition can find what they are looking for among REA's publications.

REA's practice tests are always based upon the format of the most recently administered exams, and include every type of question that can be expected on the actual exams.

REA's publications and educational materials are highly regarded and continually receive an unprecedented amount of praise from professionals, instructors, librarians, parents, and students. Our authors are as diverse as the subject matter represented in the books we publish. They are well-known in their respective disciplines and serve on the faculties of prestigious high schools, colleges, and universities throughout the United States and Canada.

Today, REA's wide-ranging catalog is a leading resource for teachers, students, and professionals. We invite you to visit us at *www.rea.com* to find out how "REA is making the world smarter."

ACKNOWLEDGMENTS

We would like to thank Pam Weston, VP, Publishing, for setting the quality standards for production integrity and managing the publication to completion; Larry B. Kling, VP, Editorial, for his editorial direction; Gianfranco Origliato for coordinating revision of the book; Diane Goldschmidt, Associate Editor, for post-production quality assurance; Christine Saul, Senior Graphic Designer, for cover design; and Network Typesetting, Inc., for typesetting the manuscript.

CONTENTS

INDEPENDENT STUDY SCHEDULE:
CLEP COLLEGE ALGEBRA CBT

This study schedule is a "road map" to help you prepare thoroughly for the CLEP College Algebra CBT. You may want to expand or condense it (the best way to do the latter is to collapse each two-week period into one) depending on how soon you'll be taking the CLEP. Be sure to set aside enough time—at least two hours a day—to study. No matter which schedule works best for you, the more time you spend studying, the more prepared and relaxed you will be on the day of the exam. We suggest that you keep at your side a blank sheet of paper and a textbook whose content parallels the exam's topical coverage. Jot down any notes or questions that come to mind while reading our review or after scoring each of your practice tests.

Week	*Activity*
1	Read Chapter 1, which introduces you to the CLEP College Algebra Computer-Based Test.
2	Take Practice Test 1 to determine your basic strengths and weaknesses. Score each section by using the scoring table in Chapter 1. You'll now have the basis for determining the areas you need to work on.
3	Carefully read Chapter 2, "Attacking Algebra Problems."
4	Carefully read our Math review, which spans all of Chapter 3.
5	Take Practice Test 2. After scoring your exam, carefully review all incorrect answer explanations. If there are any types of questions or particular subjects that seem difficult to you, review those subjects by re-reading the appropriate section(s) in this book's Chapter 2 or Chapter 3, along with the corresponding sections in your textbook.
6	Take Practice Test 3. After scoring your exam, carefully review all incorrect answer explanations. If there are any types of questions or particular subjects that seem difficult to you, review those subjects by re-reading the appropriate section(s) in this book's Chapter 2 or Chapter 3, along with the corresponding sections in your textbook.

CHAPTER 1

PASSING THE CLEP COLLEGE ALGEBRA CBT

CHAPTER 1

PASSING THE CLEP COLLEGE ALGEBRA CBT

ABOUT THIS BOOK

This book provides you with an accurate and complete representation of the CLEP College Algebra Computer-Based Test, or CBT. Inside you will find a complete review of college algebra, as well as tips and strategies for test-taking. We give you three full-length practice tests, all based on the official CLEP subject exam. Our practice tests contain every type of question that you can expect to encounter on the CLEP CBT. Following each practice test you will find an answer key with detailed explanations designed to help you more completely absorb the test material.

All 34 CLEP exams are computer-based. As you can see, the practice tests in our book are presented as paper-and-pencil exams. The content and format of the actual CLEP subject exam are faithfully mirrored. We detail the format and content of the CLEP College Algebra exam on pages 5–6.

ABOUT THE EXAM

Who takes CLEP exams and what are they used for?

CLEP (College-Level Examination Program) examinations are usually taken by adults who have acquired knowledge outside the classroom and wish to bypass certain college courses and earn college credit. The CLEP Program is designed to reward students for learning—no matter where or how that knowledge was acquired. CLEP is the most widely accepted credit-by-examination program in the United States, with over 2,900 colleges and universities granting credit for satisfactory scores on CLEP exams.

Although most CLEP examinees are adults returning to college, many graduating high school seniors, enrolled college students, and international students also take the exams to earn college credit or to demonstrate their ability to perform at the college level. There are no prerequisites, such as age or educational status, for taking CLEP examinations. However, because policies on granting credits vary among colleges, you should contact the particular institution from which you wish to receive CLEP credit.

There are two categories of CLEP examinations:

1. **CLEP General Examinations**, which are five separate tests that cover material usually taken as requirements during the first two years of college. CLEP General Examinations are available for English Composition (with or without essay), Humanities, College Mathematics, Natural Sciences, and Social Sciences and History.

2. **CLEP Subject Examinations**, which include material usually covered in an undergraduate course with a similar title. The CLEP College Algebra exam is one of 29 subject tests.

Who develops and administers the CLEP CBT exams?

The CLEP CBTs are developed by the College Board, administered by Educational Testing Service, and involve the assistance of educators throughout the U.S. The test development process is designed and carried out to ensure that the content and difficulty of the test are appropriate to the college level.

When and where is this exam given?

The CLEP College Algebra exam is offered throughout the year at about 1,000 test centers in the U.S. and can be arranged for candidates abroad on request. For details, contact the CLEP Program as follows:

CLEP Services
P.O. Box 6600
Princeton, NJ 08541-6600
Phone: (609) 771-7865
Fax: (609) 771-7088
Website: www.collegeboard.com/clep
E-mail: clep@info.collegeboard.org

Military personnel and CLEP

CLEP Exams are available free-of-charge to eligible military personnel and eligible civilian employees. The College Board has developed a paper-based version of 14 high volume/high pass rate CLEP tests for DANTES Test Centers, including Introductory Psychology. Contact the Educational Services Officer or Navy College Education Specialist for more information. Visit *www.collegeboard.com*, the official Website of the College Board, for details about CLEP opportunities for servicemembers.

HOW TO USE THIS BOOK

What do I study first?

Read over our test-format outline, test-taking tips, and course review. Then use the first practice test as a diagnostic to determine your area(s) of weakness. Once you find out where you need to spend more time, focus your efforts on those specific problem areas. To reinforce your facility with the subject matter, we advise keeping at your side a college-level textbook that covers the appropriate material.

To get the most out of your study time, follow our Independent Study Schedule located in the front of this book. The schedule is based on a six-week program but can be condensed to three weeks, if necessary, by collapsing each two-week period into one.

When should I start studying?

It's never too early to start studying for the CLEP College Algebra exam; the earlier you begin, the more time you will have to sharpen your skills. Don't leave it to the last minute; cramming is not an effective way to study, since it doesn't allow you the time needed to learn the test material.

FORMAT AND CONTENT OF THE CLEP CBT

The CLEP College Algebra CBT covers the kind of material that is typically part of a one-semester college course. Test takers can expect to encounter roughly a 50/50 split between routine and nonroutine problems—the former requiring basic algebraic skills, the latter requiring you to show your command of algebraic concepts. While you'll be able to avail yourself of an online scientific calculator (non-graphing, non-programmable) during the exam, *none* of the questions you will be asked will *require* its use. The exam will present you with 60 multiple-choice and fill-in-the-box questions to be answered in 90 minutes.

The *approximate* breakdown of topics on the CLEP College Algebra CBT is as follows:

25%   ***Algebraic Operations***

Combining algebraic expressions

Factoring

Simplifying algebraic fractions

Operating with powers and roots

20%   ***Equations, Inequalities, and their Graphs***

Linear equations and inequalities

Quadratic equations and inequalities

Systems of equations and inequalities

25%   ***Algebraic, Exponential, and Logarithmic Functions and their Graphs***

Domain

Range

Composition

Inverse of functions

30%   ***Miscellaneous Topics***

Theory of equations

Sets

Real numbers

Complex numbers

Sequences and series

PRACTICE-TEST RAW SCORE CONVERSION TABLE*

Raw Score	Scaled Score	Course Grade	Raw Score	Scaled Score	Course Grade
60	80	A	30	53	
59	80		29	52	
58	79		28	51	
57	79		27	50	C
56	78		26	49	
55	77		25	47	
54	76		24	46	
53	76		23	45	
52	75		22	44	
51	74		21	43	
50	73		20	42	
49	72		19	41	
48	71		18	40	
47	70		17	39	
46	69		16	38	
45	68		15	37	
44	67		14	36	
43	66		13	35	
42	65		12	34	
41	64		11	33	
40	63		10	32	
39	62	B	9	31	
38	61		8	30	
37	60		7	29	
36	59		6	28	
35	58		5	27	
34	57		4	26	
33	56		3	25	
32	55		2	23	
31	54		1	21	
			0	20	

*This table is provided for scoring REA practice tests only. With the advent of computer-based testing, the College-Level Examination Program uses a single across-the-board credit-granting score of 50 for all 34 CLEP computer-based exams. Nonetheless, on account of the different skills being measured and the unique content requirements of each test, the actual number of correct answers needed to reach 50 will vary. A "50" is calibrated to equate with performance that would warrant the grade C in the corresponding introductory college course.

ABOUT OUR REVIEW

Our review for the CLEP College Algebra CBT includes both a thorough rundown of the major topics found on the exam as well as hints and strategies for attacking algebra questions. The review is divided into these nine sections, corresponding to the subject matter you can expect to encounter on the CLEP exam:

1. *Sets and Set Operations*
2. *Number Systems and Fundamental Algebraic Operations*
3. *Polynomials and Rational Expressions*
4. *Equations*
5. *Inequalities*
6. *Quadratic Equations*
7. *Equations of Higher Order*
8. *Algebraic Theorems*
9. *Ratio, Proportion, and Variation*

SCORING YOUR PRACTICE TESTS

The CLEP College Algebra CBT is scored on a rights-only basis, meaning that only correct answers are scored. The conversion table on page 7 provides an estimate of your scaled score. Since scaled scores vary from one form of a test to another, your score on the actual exam may be higher or lower than what our table indicates. Again, you will suffer *no penalty* for incorrect guesses on the CLEP CBT.

When will I receive my score report and what will it look like?

The test administrator will print out a full Candidate Score Report for you immediately upon your completion of the CBT. Your scores are reported only to you, unless you ask to have them sent elsewhere. If you want your scores reported to a college or other institution, you must say so when you take the examination. Since your scores are kept on file for 20 years, you can also request transcripts from Educational Testing Service at a later date.

STUDYING FOR THE EXAM

It is crucial for you to choose the time and place for studying that works best for you. Some students set aside a certain number of hours every morning, while others choose to study at night before going to sleep. Only you can determine when and where your study time will be most effective, but be consistent and use your time wisely. Work out a study routine and stick to it!

When you take our practice tests, try to make your testing conditions as much like the actual test as possible. Turn off the television or radio, and sit down at a quiet table or desk free from distraction. Use a timer to ensure that each section is accurately clocked.

As you complete each practice test, score it and thoroughly review the explanations for the questions you answered incorrectly; but don't review too much at one sitting. Concentrate on one problem area at a time by reviewing the question and explanation, and by studying our review until you are confident that you completely understand the material.

Keep track of your scores and mark them on scratch paper. By doing so, you will be able to gauge your progress and discover general weaknesses in particular sections. You should carefully study the review sections that cover your areas of difficulty, as this will build your skills in those areas.

TEST-TAKING TIPS

You may never have taken a standardized computer-based test like the CLEP College Algebra exam, but it's not hard to learn the things you need to know to be comfortable on test day.

Know the format of the CBT. CLEP CBTs are *not adaptive* but rather fixed-length tests. In a sense, this makes them kin to the familiar paper-and-pencil exam in that you have the same flexibility to go back and review your work in each section. Moreover, the format hasn't changed a great deal from the paper-and-pencil CLEP. For this exam, you can expect to encounter 60 questions that need to be answered within 90 minutes. You are likely to see some so-called pretest, or experimental, questions as well, but you won't know which they are and they won't be scored.

Use the process of elimination. If you don't immediately see the correct answer among the choices, go down the list and eliminate as many as you can. Confidently casting aside choices will help you isolate the correct response, or at least knock your choices down to just a few strong contenders. This approach has the added benefit of keeping you from getting sidetracked and distracted by what in fact may be just an occasional tricky question. Importantly, your score is based only on the number of questions you answer *correctly*.

Work quickly and steadily. You will have 90 minutes to work on the 60 questions on the test; this means that you will want to devote an average of 90 seconds to each question. So work quickly and steadily to avoid spending an inordinate amount of time on any one question. Taking our practice tests—which, again, have a few more questions than the actual test—will help you learn to budget your time.

Learn the directions and format for each section of the test. This will put extra time on your side that you can use to review your work.

Acquaint yourself with the CBT screen. Familiarize yourself with the CLEP CBT screen beforehand by logging on to the College Board Website. Waiting until test day to see what it looks like in the pretest tutorial risks injecting needless anxiety into your testing experience.

Be sure that your answer registers before you go to the next item. Look at the screen to see that your mouse-click causes the pointer to darken the proper oval. This takes far less effort than darkening an oval on paper, but don't lull yourself into taking less care!

THE DAY OF THE EXAM

On the day of the test, you should wake up early (after a good night's rest, one would hope) and have a full breakfast. Dress comfortably so that you are not distracted by being too hot or too cold while taking the test. Plan to arrive at the test center early. This will allow you to collect your thoughts and relax before the test, and will also spare you the anxiety that comes with being late. *No one* will be allowed into the test session after the test has begun.

Before you set out for the test center, make sure that you have your admission form, Social Security number, and a photo ID with your signature (e.g., driver's license, student identification card, or current alien registration card). You need proper ID to get into the test center.

You may wear a watch to the test center, but it cannot make any noise, which could disturb your fellow test-takers. No computers, dictionaries, textbooks, notebooks, scrap paper, briefcases, or packages will be permitted; drinking, smoking, and eating are prohibited. **The use of a scientific calculator (non-graphing, non-programmable) is allowed, though as we said, one will be provided for you online. Do not bring your own.**

Good luck on the CLEP College Algebra CBT!

CHAPTER 2

ATTACKING ALGEBRA PROBLEMS

CHAPTER 2

ATTACKING ALGEBRA PROBLEMS

One of the most important rules to follow in solving any algebraic problem is to work slowly, carefully, and one step at a time. Rushing to complete an answer is a sure way to become confused and make careless errors. Be prepared for the test; this is the best way to insure that you will do your best work. Many people know the work that a test contains, yet score poorly due to nervousness. So RELAX!

A MODEL FOR PROBLEM SOLVING

A useful model for problem solving is that given to us by the mathematician Polya. It is a four-step method:

1) **Understand the question**—In order to find a correct answer, it is imperative that you understand exactly what you are being asked to find. For example, a problem may introduce a polynomial equation, such as $x^2 + 7x + 10 = 0$. The problem may require you to solve for x, or instead ask you simply to factor the equation. Knowing just what is required will save you time and unnecessary incorrect answers. Take the time to read through the entire problem before you begin working on it.

2) **Select a strategy** for finding the solution. In the above case, if the problem asks you to solve for x, look carefully at the equation $x^2 + 7x + 10 = 0$. Observe that the polynomial $x^2 + 7x + 10$ is easy to factor. Since factoring will be quicker than using the quadratic formula in this case, your best plan of attack is to solve by factoring.

3) **Solve the problem** by carrying out the plan you decided on. Work deliberately, being cautious not to miss any steps along the way. The given polynomial can be factored into the two binomials $(x + 5)$ and $(x + 2)$. Thus, $(x + 5)(x + 2) = 0$, and $x = -5$ or $x = -2$.

4) **Review your answer** and check it to be sure it is correct. You do that by substituting these values for x into the original equation,

$$x^2 + 7x + 10 = 0.$$

First, use -5:

$$(-5)^2 + 7(-5) + 10 = 0$$

$$25 + (-35) + 10 = 0$$

$$35 + (-35) = 0$$

$$0 = 0$$

You can see that -5 is a correct answer.

Now try this with -2. Again, one step at a time.

$$(-2)^2 + 7(-2) + 10 = 0$$

$$4 + (-14) + 10 = 0$$

$$14 + (-14) = 0$$

$$0 = 0$$

You can see that $x = -5$ and $x = -2$ are both correct solutions to this problem.

At first, this method may seem more complicated than simply starting to work on the problem. However, once you get used to working this way, your work will become faster, more concise, and more complete than before. You will also avoid wasting time by starting down the wrong path. Practice solving all problems by following the four-step method.

ORDER OF OPERATIONS

Another important procedure which will be of great benefit to you to remember is order of operations. These are certain rules that must be followed if you are to work correctly. If you are unsure of the correct order of operations, pay particular attention to the following:

1. All operations within parentheses are done first.

2. Next, evaluate any part of the expression which contains exponents.

3. Following this, do any multiplication and/or division from left to right.

4. Lastly, do any addition and/or subtraction, in order from left to right.

It is important to follow this order. A simple illustration will suffice to show the necessity of this procedure.

PROBLEM

Evaluate the following mathematical expression:

$$(4 - 1)^2 + 6 \times 3 - 12 \div 4 = ?$$

SOLUTION

Working strictly left to right, one would come to the following incorrect result:

$$(3)^2 + 6 \times 3 - 12 \div 4 = 9 + 6 \times 3 - 12 \div 4$$

$$= 15 \times 3 - 12 \div 4$$

$$= 45 - 12 \div 4$$

$$= 33 \div 4$$

$$= 8\frac{1}{4}$$

The correct answer, following the order of operations, is:

$$(3)^2 + 6 \times 3 - 12 \div 4 = 9 + 6 \times 3 - 12 \div 4$$

$$= 9 + 18 - 12 \div 4$$

$$= 9 + 18 - 3$$

$$= 27 - 3$$

$$= 24$$

There is a considerable difference between the two answers. Be aware of the work you are doing and the order of that work. In order to avoid confusion, there are certain accepted ways to aid the problem solver. We usually use parentheses to help ourselves. For example, in the second step above, it may be helpful for us to add parentheses if they do not appear in the original problem. You may help yourself greatly if you rewrite step 2 as follows:

$$9 + (6 \times 3) - (12 \div 4) =$$

Although the problem did not include parentheses, nothing stops you from marking them in to remind you that a particular operation should come first.

Using and Practicing Order of Operations

PROBLEM

Evaluate the algebraic expression:

$$(b^2 + 2)^2 + 3a + (4b^3 - 10) - ac$$

where $a = 6$, $b = 3$, and $c = 5$.

SOLUTION

1. Since we are given the values of a, b, and c, we can replace them in the expression, beginning with a.

   The original expression was:

   $$(b^2 + 2)^2 + 3a + (4b^3 - 10) - ac$$

   Replacing a with the numeral 6, we get:

   $$(b^2 + 2)^2 + 3 \times 6 + (4b^3 - 10) - 6 \times c$$

2. Now we replace b with 3:

   $$(3^2 + 2)^2 + 3 \times 6 + (4 \times 3^3 - 10) - 6 \times c$$

3. We replace c with its value, 5:

   $$(3^2 + 2)^2 + 3 \times 6 + (4 \times 3^3 - 10) - 6 \times 5$$

4. Remembering correct order of operations, we get:

   $$(11)^2 + 18 + (108 - 10) - 30$$

   $$121 + 18 + 98 - 30$$

   $$237 - 30 = 207$$

PROBLEM SOLVING STRATEGIES

Follow these accepted problem solving strategies:

➤ Write out the example. Don't figure it out in your head. A test is not the time to practice your mental math.

➤ Draw a picture or graph. There are times when everyone needs to draw a picture in order to organize the problem in their mind.

➤ Work backwards. Sometimes the simplest way to solve a problem is by beginning with the answer choices.

➤ Make a list. Another way to organize your thoughts is by making a list of the data presented in the problem.

➤ "Guess and Check" is a useful strategy when there seems to be no example to write or operation to perform. Estimate and get as close to an answer as you can. Then check your answer with the original problem. If not quite correct, adjust your answer accordingly.

➤ Use a simpler, but related problem. Sometimes we get confused, frightened, or just put off by the sheer complexity of the numbers in a problem.

PROBLEM

Will the sum of the consecutive odd positive numbers from 31 to 59 be odd or even?

SOLUTION

Some people may immediately start this problem by writing $31 + 33 + 35 + 37\ldots$. But if you glance again at the problem, all we are asked is whether the sum will be odd or even. An easier and much quicker method of finding the answer would be to look at simpler numbers:

$$1 + 3 + 5 = 9, 3 + 5 + 7 = 15, 7 + 9 + 11 = 27, \text{etc.}$$

We can see that any time we add an odd number of odd numbers, the sum will be odd. We need go no further.

TYPES OF PROBLEMS

Now that you know how to approach the kinds of math problems you will find on the CLEP: College Algebra, let's look at each specific type of question and how to approach it.

Composition of Two Functions

PROBLEM

Let $f(x) = x^2 + 6$, $g(x) = 2x^2$. Solve for $f(g(x))$.

(A) $4x^2 + 12$ (D) $2x^4 + 12x^2$

(B) $4x^4 + 6$ (E) $2x^3 + 12x$

(C) $6x^2 + 2$

SOLUTION

1. We are given $g(x) = 2x^2$. Thus, we can substitute $2x^2$ for $g(x)$ in the expression $f(g(x))$:

   $$f(g(x)) = f(2x^2)$$

   Now to complete the problem, we are required to find $f(2x^2)$.

2. We are given $f(x) = x^2 + 6$. How do we find $f(2x^2)$? This is done by substituting $2x^2$ for x in the function $f(x)$. A few simpler substitutions will make the process clear:

3. Do not confuse $f(g(x))$ with $f(x)g(x)$; these two notations mean very different things. The first indicates a composite function, while the second indicates that two functions are to be multiplied together.

   $$f(x) = x^2 + 6$$
   $$f(a) = a^2 + 6$$
   $$f(7) = 7^2 + 6$$

Thus, $\ f(2x^2) = (2x^2)^2 + 6$

$$= 2^2 x^4 + 6$$

$$= 4x^4 + 6$$

We have just shown that $f(g(x)) = f(2x^2) = 4x^4 + 6$, so the correct answer is (B).

Notes: $f(g(x))$ (pronounced "f of g of x") is called a composite function. An alternate notation for $f(g(x))$ is $(f \circ g)(x)$. As we saw in the example above, a composite function is formed when one function is substituted into another function.

Solving Quadratic Equations

PROBLEM

Solve for x, when $x^2 + 2 = 3x$

(A) $(-3, 2)$ (D) $(1, 2)$

(B) $(2, -1)$ (E) $(1, -3)$

(C) $(4, 6)$

SOLUTION

1. Look at the equation. Does there seem to be a simple algebraic solution? If not, what method should we use to find a solution?

2. We will have to solve this as a quadratic equation.

3. In order to do this, first move all values to one side, leaving only zero on the other side.

4. We must add $-3x$ (subtract $3x$) to both sides.

$$x^2 + 2 = 3x$$
$$-3x = -3x$$

The resulting equation is $x^2 - 3x + 2 = 0$

5. We must now factor $x^2 - 3x + 2$. The two binomials which result are:

$(x - 2)$ and $(x - 1)$

We set these two factors equal to 0 and get:

$(x - 2)(x - 1) = 0$

6. Now separate the two factors, such that $x - 2 = 0$ and $x - 1 = 0$. The resulting answers are: $x = 2$ and $x = 1$.

7. In order to check these answers, substitute these values for x in the original equation.

$$x^2 + 2 = 3x$$

If $x = 1$, then $1^2 + 2 = 3 \times 1$

$$1 + 2 = 3$$
$$3 = 3$$

If $x = 2$, then $2^2 + 2 = 3 \times 2$

$$4 + 2 = 6$$
$$6 = 6$$

We can see that both $x = 1$ and $x = 2$ satisfy the equation, so the answer is (D).

Note: If a quadratic equation cannot be factored, or if you are having difficulty finding the factors, use the quadratic formula:

$$x = \frac{-b \pm \sqrt{b^2 - 4ac}}{2a}$$

Graphing Equations

PROBLEM

Which of these points appears in the intersection of $y \geq x^2$ and $0 \leq y \leq 4$?

(A) $(-1.75, 4)$ (D) $(1.75, -4)$

(B) $(3, 3)$ (E) $(2, -4)$

(C) $(0, 2)$

SOLUTION

The most effective way to solve the problem is to graph it. But first, ask yourself "what must I do before I can make the graphs?" You should make a chart that will show the coordinates of several points on the graph.

1. Evaluate $y = x^2$. Square each value of x to find the related value of y. Chart the coordinates of $y = x^2$, and draw the corresponding graph.

x	y
-4	16
-3	9
-2	4
-1	1
0	0
1	1
2	4
3	9
4	16

2. Shade the region above the parabola in order to represent the inequality $y \geq x^2$ (points on the parabola are also solutions to this inequality, so they are considered to be part of the shaded region).

3. Shade the region between the lines $y = 0$ and $y = 4$, to represent the inequality $0 \leq y \leq 4$ (points on these lines are also solutions to this inequality, so they are considered to be part of the shaded region).

4. The overlap of the two shaded regions gives the intersection of $y \geq x^2$ and $0 \leq y \leq 4$. Our point must lie within this overlap region. Of the given choices, only the point $(-1.75, 4)$ is found there, so the answer is (A).

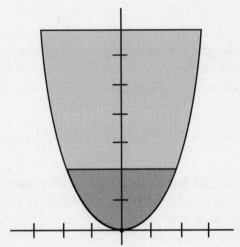

Finding Cube Roots

PROBLEM

What is the cube root of $27a^9 b^3$?

(A) $3ab^3$ (D) $6a^2b$

(B) $6a^3b$ (E) $3a^3b$

(C) $9a^3b$

SOLUTION

1. Look carefully at the problem and note what you are being asked to find. The answer must be the *cube* root of the expression given.

2. To find a cube root, it is important to remember that

$$\sqrt[3]{27a^9b^3}$$

is equivalent to

$$\sqrt[3]{27} \times \sqrt[3]{a^9} \times \sqrt[3]{b^3}$$

3. This being the case, you can take each term separately and find its cube root. The result is:

    $3 \times a^3 \times b = 3a^3b$. Therefore, (E) is correct.

    Cube roots may also be used in solving volume word problems, such as:

PROBLEM

Robert has a cube-shaped storage box where he keeps swimming pool supplies. The storage box has a volume of 125 cubic meters. What is the length of one side of the cube?

```
┌─────────────┐
│             │
└─────────────┘
```

SOLUTION

1. Question yourself as to what you are being asked to find. How can you find the volume of a cube? If you know the volume, how do you find the length of a side? Volume is equal to the length times the width times the height:

    $V = l \times w \times h$.

    Since the figure in the problem is a cube, each of those measures will be the same, so

    $V = $ side $\times$ side $\times$ side, or s^3.

2. Since we already know the volume and seek to find the measure of the sides, we use the inverse of the formula: side = cube root of volume, or

    $$s = \sqrt[3]{125}$$

3. The cube root of 125 is 5, so each side of the cube will measure 5 meters. Enter 5 in the answer box.

Operations on Polynomials

Remember that when you multiply factors with the same base, you multiply their coefficients, but add their exponents, e.g., $a^4 \times 3a^2 \times 2a^3 = $

$6a^9$. When no coefficient is shown, it is assumed to be 1. When you divide factors with the same base, you divide their coefficients, but subtract their exponents.

PROBLEM

What will be the product if you multiply

$(x^4 + 2x^2 - 6x + 4)$ by $(3x^2)$?

(A) $3x^8 + 6x^4 - 18x^2 + 12$

(D) $3x^6 - 6x + 12$

(B) $3x^6 + 6x^4 - 18x^3 + 12x^2$

(E) $12x^6 - 6x^4 + 18x^2 - 12x$

(C) $6x^6 + 6x^4 - 12x^2 + 12$

SOLUTION

Look at the answer choices. In choice (A), the first term is $3x^8$. If you multiply x^2 by x^4, will you get x^8? The answer to that is clearly NO. You don't multiply the exponents, you add them. You would get x^6. We know immediately that (A) is incorrect.

Answer (E) does show x^6 as its first term, but somehow you would have to get $12x^6$ and that is clearly wrong. If you multiply the coefficients, you get $1 \times 3 = 3$. So (C) is also wrong.

Answer (D) only shows three terms and you know the answer must have four terms. The answer, by process of elimination, must be (B).

Here is another method of solving the problem. You can break this example down into four simpler problems: Using the distributive property of multiplication, you would get these four results:

$$(3x^2 \times x^4) = 3x^6$$

$$(3x^2 \times 2x^2) = 6x^4$$

$$(3x^2 \times -6x) = -18x^3$$

$$(3x^2 \times 4) = 12x^2$$

So, those are the four terms of your answer. Putting them together, you get $3x^6 + 6x^4 - 18x^3 + 12x^2$—answer choice (B).

As you can see, this question can be solved in two legitimate ways. In the first solution, we didn't seek an exact product. Instead, we tried to eliminate answer choices by finding even one simple mistake. In the second method, we broke the equation down into its four terms and multiplied each term by $3x^2$. Then we recombined terms and again found answer (B) to be correct.

Remember: Both methods are fine. You are looking for the correct answer, and there is often more than one road to lead you there.

Simplifying Fractions Which Contain Radicals

PROBLEM

The fraction $\dfrac{\sqrt{50} - 15}{5}$ in simplest form is equal to

(A) 7.

(D) $\sqrt{2} - 3$.

(B) $\dfrac{2\sqrt{2}}{5}$.

(E) $\dfrac{22}{\sqrt{5}}$.

(C) $2\sqrt{3} - 2$.

SOLUTION

1. In order to simplify the fraction and solve this problem, we will make use of fundamental properties of fractions, radicals, multiplication, and division. We know that $\sqrt{50}$ can be written as $(\sqrt{25} \times \sqrt{2})$, and we know that we can write 15 as (3×5), so we can now rewrite our expression this way:

$$\frac{(\sqrt{25} \times \sqrt{2}) - (5 \times 3)}{5}$$

Since $\sqrt{25} = 5$, we can again rewrite the example.

$$\frac{(5\sqrt{2}) - (5 \times 3)}{5}$$

We can factor out the 5 and re-write:

$$\frac{5(\sqrt{2} - 3)}{5}$$

The 5 in the numerator and the 5 in the denominator cancel each other, leaving us:

$\sqrt{2} - 3$, answer choice (D).

Systems of Linear Equations

Look at the two linear equations $x + y = 5$ and $x - y = 1$. The two equations, when considered together, form a system of equations. To solve this system means to find a solution which satisfies both equations simultaneously. Graphically, our solution will be the one point where the two lines intersect. This point will have coordinates (x, y) which we must find as follows. First, add the two equations in order to eliminate y.

$$x + y = 5$$
$$x - y = 1$$
$$2x = 6$$
$$x = 3$$

Substituting 3 for x, we solve for y:

$$3 + y = 5, \text{ so } y = 2.$$

Substituting 3 for x and 2 for y in the two equations, we see the answers are correct.

Note: A system of two linear equations in two unknowns may have:

(1) One solution. This will be the intersection point, (x, y), as in the example above.

(2) No solution. If a system contains two parallel lines, there will be no intersection, and thus no solution.

(3) An infinite number of solutions. (Coinciding lines.)

These are the only possibilities when you have two linear equations in two unknowns.

KEYWORDS

The most difficult part of solving a word problem can be knowing how to set up the necessary equations. You can do this more easily if you learn to recognize keywords. Keywords are words or phrases that tell how quantities in a problem are related. They provide clues that help you translate sentences into questions. Listed below are some common keywords and the type of mathematical action they indicate.

Keyword	Action
sum; more than; greater than	add
difference; less than; smaller than	subtract
of	multiply
half of	divide by 2
twice as much; twice as great	multiply by 2
is; was; will be; total	equals

PROBLEM

The difference between two positive integers is 15. The smaller number is $\frac{1}{6}$ of the larger number. What is the value of the smaller number?

(A) 1

(B) 3

(C) 6

(D) 9

(E) 12

SOLUTION

The first sentence contains keywords *difference* and *is*. Assigning the variables x and y to the unknown numbers, you can write: $x - y = 15$.

The second sentence contains keywords *is* and *of*. This sentence becomes $y = (\frac{1}{6})x$.

Solving the two equations by substitution, you obtain: $x = 18$ and $y = 3$. The correct answer is (B).

Be cautious with the use of keywords. Whereas they can help you, they can also be used to deceive you. A clever test writer will use keywords in ways that will not necessarily be the same as ways we normally use them. For example, the terms "more than" and "greater than" are often used to signal addition, as in this question: Peter has $1.95. Paul has $3.17 more than that. How much money does Paul have? You can immediately see the need to add. But now look at the same keyword used in a slightly different way: Peter has $1.95. Paul has $3.17. How much more money does Paul have than Peter? Here the strategy would clearly be to subtract. The blind use of keywords can lead you astray.

CHAPTER 3

MATH REVIEW

CHAPTER 3

MATH REVIEW

SETS AND SET OPERATIONS

Sets

A set is defined as a collection of items. Each individual item belonging to a set is called an element or member of that set. Sets are usually represented by capital letters, elements by lowercase letters. If an item k belongs to a set A, we write $k \, \varepsilon \, A$ ("k is an element of A"). If k is not in A, we write $k \notin A$ ("k is not an element of A"). The order of the elements in a set does not matter:

$$\{1, 2, 3\} = \{3, 2, 1\} = \{1, 3, 2\}, \text{etc.}$$

A set can be described in two ways: 1) it can be listed element by element, or 2) a rule characterizing the elements in a set can be formulated. For example, given the set A of the whole numbers starting with 1 and ending with 9, we can describe it either as $A = \{1, 2, 3, 4, 5, 6, 7, 8, 9\}$ or as {the set of whole numbers greater than 0 and less than 10}. In both methods, the description is enclosed in brackets. A kind of shorthand is often used for the second method of set description; instead of writing out a complete sentence in between the brackets, we write instead

$$A = \{k \mid 0 < k < 10, k \text{ a whole number}\}.$$

This is read as "the set of all elements k such that k is greater than 0 and less than 10, where k is a whole number."

A set not containing any members is called the empty or null set. It is written either as ϕ or $\{ \ \}$.

Subsets

Given two sets A and B, A is said to be a subset of B if every member of set A is also a member of set B. A is a *proper* subset of B if B contains at least one element not in A. We write $A \subseteq B$ if A is a subset of B, and $A \subset B$ if A is a proper subset of B. For example, let

$$A = \{1, 2, 3, 4, 5\}$$
$$B = \{1, 2\}$$
$$C = \{1, 4, 2, 3, 5\}$$

Then 1) A equals C, and A and C are subsets of each other, but not proper subsets and 2) $B \subseteq A, B \subseteq C, B \subset A, B \subset C$. ($B$ is a subset of both A and C. In particular, B is a proper subset of A and C.)

Union and Intersection of Sets

A universal set U is a set from which other sets draw their members. If A is a subset of U, then the complement of A, denoted A' (or A^0), is the set of all elements in the universal set that are not elements of A. For example, if

$$U = \{1, 2, 3, 4, 5, 6, \dots\} \text{ and } A = \{1, 2, 3\}, \text{ then } A' = \{4, 5, 6, \dots\}.$$

The figure below illustrates this concept through the use of a *Venn diagram*.

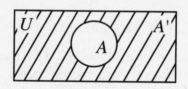

The union of two sets A and B, denoted $A \cup B$, is the set of all elements that are either in A or B or both.

The intersection of two sets A and B, denoted $A \cap B$, is the set of all elements that belong to both A and B.

If $A = \{1, 2, 3, 4, 5\}$ and $B = \{2, 3, 4, 5, 6\}$ then $A \cup B = \{1, 2, 3, 4, 5, 6\}$ and $A \cap B = \{2, 3, 4, 5\}$.

If $A \cap B, = \phi$, A and B are *disjoint*. The two figures below are Venn diagrams for union and intersection. The shaded areas represent the given operation.

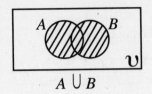

$A \cup B$

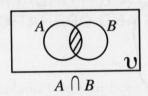

$A \cap B$

Laws of Set Operations

If U is the universal set and A is *any* subset of U, then the following hold for union, intersection, and complement:

Identity Laws

1a. $A \cup \phi = A$

1b. $A \cap \phi = \phi$

2a. $A \cup U = U$

2b. $A \cap U = A$

Idempotent Laws

3a. $A \cup A = A$

3b. $A \cap A = A$

Complement Laws

4a. $A \cup A' = U$

4b. $A \cap A' = \phi$

5a. $(A') = A$

5b. $\phi' = U; U' = \phi$

Commutative Laws

6a. $A \cup B = B \cup A$

6b. $A \cap B = B \cap A$

Associative Laws

7a. $(A \cup B) \cup C = A \cup (B \cup C)$

7b. $(A \cap B) \cap C = A \cap (B \cap C)$

Distributive Laws

8a. $A \cup (B \cap C) = (A \cup B) \cap (A \cup C)$

8b. $A \cap (B \cup C) = (A \cap B) \cup (A \cap C)$

DeMorgan's Laws

9a. $(A \cup B)' = A' \cap B'$ 9b. $(A \cap B)' = A' \cup B'$

NUMBER SYSTEMS AND FUNDAMENTAL ALGEBRAIC LAWS AND OPERATIONS

Number Systems

Most of the numbers used in algebra belong to a set called the real numbers, or reals. This set, denoted R, can be represented graphically by the real number line.

Given a straight horizontal line extending continuously in both directions, we arbitrarily fix a point and label it with the number 0. In a similar manner, we can label any point on the line with one of the real numbers, depending on its position relative to 0. Numbers to the right of zero are called positive, while those to the left are called negative. Value increases from left to right, so that if a is to the right of b, it is said to be greater than b.

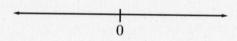

$$0$$

Integers

If we divide the number line into equal segments called unit lengths, we can then label the boundary points of these segments according to their distance from zero. For example, the point 2 lengths to the left of zero is -2, while the point 3 lengths to the right of zero is $+3$ (the + sign is usually assumed, so +3 is written as 3). The number line now looks like this:

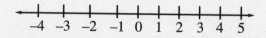

$$-4 \quad -3 \quad -2 \quad -1 \quad 0 \quad 1 \quad 2 \quad 3 \quad 4 \quad 5$$

These boundary points represent the subset of the reals known as the integers, denoted Z. Some subsets of Z are the natural numbers or positive integers, the set of integers starting with 1 and increasing, $Z^+ = N = \{1, 2, 3, 4...\}$; the whole numbers, the set of integers starting with 0 and increasing, $W = \{0, 1, 2, 3,...\}$; the negative integers, the set of integers starting with –1 and decreasing: $Z^- = \{-1, -2, -3,...\}$; and the prime numbers, the set of positive integers greater than 1 that are divisible only by 1 and themselves: $\{2, 3, 5, 7, 11,...\}$.

Rationals

One of the main subsets of the reals is the set of rational numbers, denoted Q. This set is defined as all the numbers that can be expressed in the form a/b, where a and b are integers, $b \neq 0$. This form is called a fraction or ratio; a is known as the numerator, b the denominator. For example,

$$\frac{-7}{5}, \frac{8}{6}, \frac{9}{-3}, \frac{5}{100}$$

Note: The integers can all be expressed in the form a/b. For example,

$$2 = \frac{2}{1}, \; -3 = \frac{6}{-2}, \; -5 = \frac{-5}{1}$$

Irrationals

The complement of the set of rationals is the irrationals, whose symbol is Q'. For now, they are defined as the set of real numbers that cannot be expressed in the form

$$\frac{a}{b}, b \neq 0.$$

Absolute Value

The absolute value of a real number A is defined as follows:

$$|A| = \begin{cases} A \text{ if } A \geq 0 \\ -A \text{ if } A < 0 \end{cases}$$

For example, $|5| = 5, |-8| = -(-8) = 8$.

Absolute values follow the given rules:

A) $|-A| = |A|$

B) $|A| \geq 0$, equality holding only if $A = 0$

C) $\left|\dfrac{A}{B}\right| = \dfrac{|A|}{|B|}, B \neq 0$

D) $|AB| = |A| \times |B|$

E) $|A|^2 = A^2$

Absolute value can also be expressed on the real number line as the distance of the point represented by the real number from the point labeled 0.

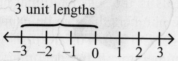

So $|-3| = 3$ because -3 is 3 units to the left of 0.

Fundamental Algebraic Laws

Note that $a, b, c \, \varepsilon R$.

A) **Closure Law of Addition**

The sum of two real numbers is always a real number.

$a + b = c$

B) **Closure Law of Multiplication**

The product of two real numbers is always a real number.

$a \times b = c$

C) **Commutative Law of Addition**

$a + b = b + a$

Commutative refers to position. The sum of two real numbers is the same even if their positions are changed. For example,

$3 + 2 = 5 = 2 + 3$

D) **Commutative Law of Multiplication**

$a \times b = b \times a$

The product of two real numbers is the same even if their positions are changed. For example,

$3 \times 2 = 6 = 2 \times 3$

E) **Associative Law of Addition**

$$(a + b) + c = a + (b + c)$$

Associative refers to grouping. The sum of any three real numbers is the same regardless of the way they are grouped. For example,

$$(5 + 3) + 2 = 10 = 5 + (3 + 2)$$

F) **Associative Law of Multiplication**

$$(a \times b) \times c = a \times (b \times c)$$

The product of any three real numbers is the same, regardless of the way they are grouped. For example,

$$(5 \times 3) \times 2 = 30 = 5 \times (3 \times 2)$$

G) **Additive Identity**

There exists a real number 0 such that $a + 0 = a$. The number 0 is referred to as the additive identity.

H) **Multiplicative Identity**

There exists a real number 1 such that $a \times 1 = a$. The number 1 is referred to as the multiplicative identity.

I) **Additive Inverse**

For each real number a, there is a unique real number $-a$, called the additive inverse of a, such that $a + (-a) = 0$. For example,

$$7 + (-7) = 0$$

J) **Multiplicative Inverse**

For every real number a, where $a \neq 0$, there is a unique real number

$$\frac{1}{a},$$

called the multiplicative inverse of a, such that

$$a \times \frac{1}{a} = 1.$$

For example,

$$7 \times \frac{1}{7} = 1$$

K) **Zero Law**

For every number a, $a \times 0 = 0$.

L) **Distributive Law for Multiplication With Respect to Addition and Subtraction**

$a(b + c) = ab + ac$

$\qquad = ba + ca \qquad$ by the commutative law

$\qquad = (b + c)a$

also $a(b - c) = ab - ac$

$\qquad\qquad = ba - ca$

$\qquad\qquad = (b - c)a$

For example,

1) $3(4 + 5) = 3(4) + 3(5)$

$\qquad\qquad = (4)3 + (5)3 = (4 + 5)3 = 27$

2) $3(5 - 4) = 3(5) - 3(4)$

$\qquad\qquad = (5)3 - (4)3 = (5 - 4)3 = 3$

These rules also hold for certain subsets of the reals R, such as the rationals Q. They do not hold for all subsets of R, however; for instance, the integers Z do not contain multiplicative inverses for integers other than 1 or -1.

Basic Algebraic Operations

A) To add two numbers with like signs, add their absolute values and prefix the sum with the common sign. For example,

$6 + 2 = 8$, $(-6) + (-2) = -8$

B) To add two numbers with unlike signs, find the difference between their absolute values, and prefix the result with the sign of the number with the greater absolute value. For example,

$(-4) + 6 = 2$, $15 + (-19) = -4$

C) To subtract a number b from another number a, change the sign of b and add to a. For example,

(1) $10 - 3 = 10 + (-3) = 7$

(2) $2 - (-6) = 2 + 6 = 8$

(3) $(-5) - (-2) = -5 + (+2) = -3$

D) To multiply (or divide) two numbers having like signs, multiply (or divide) their absolute values and prefix the result with a positive sign. For example,

(1) $(5)(3) = 15$

(2) $\dfrac{-6}{-3} = 2$

E) To multiply (or divide) two numbers having unlike signs, multiply (or divide) their absolute values and prefix the result with a negative sign. For example,

(1) $(-2)(8) = -16$

(2) $\dfrac{9}{-3} = -3$

Operations with Fractions

To understand the operations on fractions, it is first desirable to understand what is known as factoring.

The product of two numbers is equal to a unique number. The two numbers are said to be factors of the unique number and the process of finding the two numbers is called factoring. It is important to note that when a number in a particular set is factored, then the factors of the number are also in the same set.

For example, the factors of 6 are

(1) 1 and 6, since $1 \times 6 = 6$

(2) 2 and 3, since $2 \times 3 = 6$.

A) The value of a fraction remains unchanged, if its numerator and denominator are both multiplied or divided by the same number, other than zero. For example,

$$\frac{1}{2} \times \frac{2}{2} = \frac{2}{4} = \frac{1}{2}$$

This is because a fraction $\dfrac{b}{b}$, b being any number, is equal to the multiplicative identity, 1.

B) To simplify a fraction is to convert it into a form in which the numerator and denominator have no common factor other than 1. For example,

$$\frac{50}{25} = \frac{50 \div 25}{25 \div 25}$$

$$= \frac{2}{1} = 2$$

C)   The algebraic sum of the fractions having a common denominator is a fraction whose numerator is the algebraic sum of the numerators of the given fractions and whose denominator is the common denominator. For example,

$$\frac{11}{3} + \frac{5}{3} = \frac{11+5}{3} = \frac{16}{3}$$

Similarly, for subtraction

$$\frac{11}{3} - \frac{5}{3} = \frac{11-5}{3} = \frac{6}{3} = 2$$

D)   To find the sum of two fractions having different denominators, it is necessary to find the lowest common denominator (LCD) of the different denominators and convert the fractions into equivalent fractions having the lowest common denominator as a denominator. For example,

$$\frac{11}{6} + \frac{5}{16} = ?$$

To find the LCD, we must first find the prime factors of the two denominators.

$$6 = 2 \times 3$$

$$16 = 2 \times 2 \times 2 \times 2$$

$$LCD = 2 \times 2 \times 2 \times 2 \times 3 = 48$$

Note that we do not need to repeat the 2 that appears in both the factors of 6 and 16.

We now rewrite $^{11}/_6$ and $^5/_{16}$ to have 48 as their denominator.

$$\frac{11}{6} \times \frac{8}{8} = \frac{88}{48}$$

$$\frac{5}{16} \times \frac{3}{3} = \frac{15}{48}$$

We may now apply rule 3 to find

$$\frac{11}{6} + \frac{15}{16} = \frac{103}{48}$$

E)   The product of two or more fractions produces a fraction whose numerator is the product of the numerators of the given fractions and whose denominator is the product of the denominators of the given fractions. For example,

$$\frac{2}{3} \times \frac{1}{5} \times \frac{4}{7} = \frac{8}{105}$$

F)   The quotient of two given fractions is obtained by inverting the divisor and then multiplying. For example,

$$\frac{8}{9} \div \frac{1}{3} = \frac{8}{9} \times \frac{3}{1} = \frac{8}{3}$$

Decimals

If we divide the denominator of a fraction into its numerator, we obtain a decimal form for it. This form attaches significance to the placement of an integer relative to a decimal point. The first place to the left of the decimal point is the units place; the second to the left, is the tens; third, the hundreds, etc. The first place to the right of the decimal point is the tenths, the second the hundredths, etc. The integer in each place tells how many of the values of that place the given number has.

EXAMPLE

721 has seven hundreds, two tens, and one unit. .584 has five tenths, eight hundredths, and four thousandths.

Since a rational number is of the form $^a/_b$, where $b \neq 0$, all rational numbers can be expressed as decimals by dividing b into a. The resulting decimal is either a terminating decimal, meaning that b divides a with reminder 0 after a certain point; or repeating, meaning that b continues to divide a so that the decimal has a repeating pattern of integers. For example,

A) $\frac{1}{2} = .5$

B) $\frac{1}{3} = .333...$

C) $\dfrac{11}{16} = .6875$

D) $\dfrac{2}{7} = .285714285714....$

A) and C) are terminating decimals; B) and D) are repeating decimals. This explanation allows us to define irrational numbers as numbers whose decimal form is nonterminating and nonrepeating. For example,

$$\sqrt{2} = 1.414...$$

$$\sqrt{3} = 1.732....$$

So the set of reals is the union of the set of rationals and the set of irrationals ($R = Q \cup Q'$).

IMAGINARY AND COMPLEX NUMBERS

Imaginary Numbers

If a number a is multiplied by itself to produce a new number b, b is called the square of a and a the square root of b, denoted $a = \sqrt{b}$. For example,

$$3 \times 3 = 9, \quad \sqrt{9} = 3$$

3^2, read "3 to the second power" or "3 squared," indicates that 3 is to be used as a factor of the expression 3^2, i.e., $3^2 = 3 \times 3$.

According to the law of signs for real numbers, the square of a positive or negative number is always positive. This means that it is impossible to take the square root of a negative number in the real number system. In order to make this possible, the symbol i is defined as $i \equiv \sqrt{-1}$, $i^2 = -1$. i is called an imaginary number, as is any multiple of i by a real number. This set is denoted R'.

Complex Numbers (C)

A complex number is a combination of real and imaginary numbers of the form $a + bi$, where a and b are real and i is defined as above. a is called the real part while b is called the imaginary part of $a + bi$.

Both the real and the imaginary number set are subsets of C. $R = \{a + bi \mid b = 0\}$ and $R' = \{a + bi \mid a = 0\}$. Of the figures below the first uses a

Venn diagram to illustrate the relationships of the various number systems to each other, while the second uses the tree form.

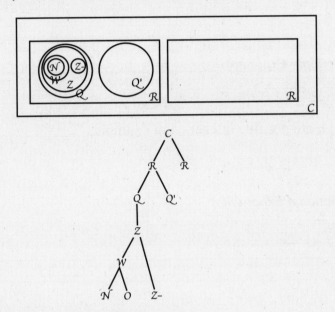

EXPONENTS AND RADICALS

Exponents

Given the expression $a^n = b$, where a, n, and b ε R, a is called the base, n is called the exponent or power.

For example, in 3^2, 3 is the base, 2 is the exponent. If n is a positive integer and if x and y are real numbers such that $x^n = y$, then x is said to be an nth root of y, written

$$x = \sqrt[n]{y} = y^{1/n}$$

Positive Integral Exponent

If n is a positive integer, then a^n represents the product of n factors each of which is a.

Negative Integral Exponent

If n is a positive integer,

$$a^{-n} = \frac{1}{a^n} \quad a \neq 0$$

For example,

$$2^{-4} = \frac{1}{2^n} = \frac{1}{16}$$

Positive Fractional Exponent

$$a^{m/n} = \sqrt[n]{a^m}$$

where m and n are positive integers. For example,

$$4^{3/2} = \sqrt[2]{4^3} = \sqrt{64} = 8$$

Negative Fractional Exponent

$$a^{-m/n} = \frac{1}{a^{m/n}}$$

For example,

$$27^{-2/3} = \frac{1}{27^{2/3}} = \frac{1}{\sqrt[3]{27^2}} = \frac{1}{\sqrt[3]{729}} = \frac{1}{9}$$

Zero Exponent

$$a^0 = 1, a \neq 0$$

General Laws of Exponents

A) $a^p a^q = a^{p+q}$

B) $(a^p)^q = a^{pq}$

C) $\dfrac{a^p}{a^q} = a^{p-q}, a \neq 0$

D) $(ab)^p = a^p b^p$

E) $\left(\dfrac{a}{b}\right)^p = \dfrac{a^p}{b^p}, b \neq 0$

Radicals

A radical is an expression of the form $\sqrt[n]{a}$ which denotes the nth root of a positive integer a; n is the index of the radical and the number a is the radicand. The index is usually omitted if $n = 2$.

Laws for radicals are the same as laws for exponents, since

$$\sqrt[n]{a} = a^{\frac{1}{n}}, n \neq 0$$

Some of these laws are:

A) $\left(\sqrt[n]{a}\right)^n = a$

B) $\sqrt[n]{ab} = \sqrt[n]{a}\sqrt[n]{b}$

C) $\sqrt[n]{a/b} = \sqrt[n]{a} / \sqrt[n]{b}, \quad b \neq 0$

D) $\sqrt[n]{a^m} = \left(\sqrt[n]{a}\right)^m$

E) $\sqrt[m]{\sqrt[n]{a}} = \sqrt[mn]{a}$

A radical is said to be in simplest form if:

A) All perfect nth powers have been removed from the radical. For example,

$$\sqrt[3]{8x^5} = \sqrt[3]{(2x)^3 \times x^2} = 2x\left(\sqrt[3]{x^2}\right).$$

B) The index of the radical is as small as possible.

C) There aren't any fractions present in the radicand.

Two radicals are said to be similar if they have the same index and the same radicand.

To algebraically add or subtract two or more radicals, reduce each given radical to the simplest form, and add or subtract terms with the same radicals. For example,

$$\sqrt{27} + \sqrt{12} = \sqrt{3^2 \times 3} + \sqrt{2^2 \times 3} = 3\sqrt{3} + 2\sqrt{3} = 5\sqrt{3}$$

To multiply two or more radicals with the same radicands, write the radicals in the form a^x, then apply the law

$$a^x a^y = a^{x+y}.$$

For example,

$$\sqrt{27} + \sqrt{12} = \sqrt{3^3 \times 3} + \sqrt{2^2 \times 3} = 3\sqrt{3} + 2\sqrt{3} = 5\sqrt{3}$$

$$\sqrt{2}\sqrt[5]{2}(3\sqrt{2})^4 = 2^{\left(\frac{1}{2}+\frac{1}{5}+\frac{4}{3}\right)} = 2^{\frac{61}{30}} = \sqrt[30]{2^{61}}$$

To divide two radicals with the same radicands, write the radicals in the form a^x, then apply the law

$$\frac{a^x}{a^y} = a^{x-y}.$$

For example,

$$\left(\sqrt{5}\right) \div \left(\sqrt[3]{5}\right) = (5^{\frac{1}{2}}) \div (5^{\frac{1}{3}})$$
$$= 5^{\left(\frac{1}{2}-\frac{1}{3}\right)} = 5^{\frac{1}{6}}$$
$$= \sqrt[6]{5}$$

Scientific Notation

A real number expressed in scientific notation is written as a product of a real number n and an integral power of 10; the value of n is $1 \le n < 10$. For example,

	Number	Scientific Notation
1)	1956.	1.956×10^3
2)	.0036	3.6×10^{-3}
3)	59600000.	5.96×10^7

POLYNOMIALS AND RATIONAL EXPRESSIONS

Terms and Expressions

A *variable* is defined as a placeholder, which can take on any of several values at a given time; it is usually represented by one of the last letters of the alphabet such as x, y, and z. A *constant* is a symbol which takes on only one value at a given time. If the value of the constant is unknown, it is usually denoted by the letters a, b, or c. $\pi, 5, 8/17$, and $-i$ are constants.

A *term* is a constant, a variable, a product of constants and variables, a quotient of constants and variables, or a combination of products and quotients. For example, 7.76, $3x$, xyz, $x/5$, $5z/x$, and $(0.99)x^2$ are terms. If a term is a combination of constants and variables, the constant part of the term is referred to as the *coefficient* of the variable. If a variable is written without a coefficient, the coefficient is assumed to be 1. For example,

$3x^2$ $y^3 = (1)y^3$
coefficient: 3   coefficient: 1
variable: x variable: y

An *expression* is a collection of one or more terms. If the number of terms is greater than 1, the expression is said to be the sum of terms. For example,

$9, 9xy, 6x + x/3, 8yz - 2x$

The Polynomial

An algebraic expression consisting of only one term is called a *monomial*. An algebraic expression consisting of two terms is called a *binomial*. An algebraic expression consisting of three terms is called a *trinomial*. In general, an algebraic expression consisting of two or more terms is called a *multinomial*.

A *polynomial in x,* denoted $P(x)$, consists of one or more terms such that the terms are either an integral constant or the product of an integral constant and a positive integral power of x. For example,

$5x^3 + 2x^2 + 3$ is a polynomial in x.

$2x^2 + x^{\frac{1}{2}} - 1$ is not a polynomial in x.

$9x^3 + 3x^{-2} + 4$ is not a polynomial in x.

The degree of a monomial is the sum of the exponents of the variables. The degree of a monomial with no variables is 0. For example,

$5x^2$ has degree 2.

$3x^3y^2z$ has degree 6.

9 has degree 0.

The degree of a polynomial is equal to the exponent of that term with the highest power of x whose coefficient is not 0. For example,

$5x^4 + 7x + 12$ has degree 4.

Algebraic Operations with Polynomials

Addition of polynomials is achieved by combining like terms, defined as terms which differ only in numerical coefficients. For example,

$(x^2 - 3x + 5) + (4x^2 + 6x - 3)$

Note: Parenthesis are used to distinguish polynomials.

By using the commutative and associative laws, we can rewrite $P(x)$ as:

$$P(x) = (x^2 + 4x^2) + (6x - 3x) + (5 - 3)$$

Using the distributive law yields

$$(1 + 4)x^2 + (6 - 3)x + (5 - 3) = 5x^2 + 3x + 2$$

Subtraction of two polynomials is achieved by first changing the sign of all terms in the expression which is being subtracted and then adding this result to the other expression. For example,

$$(5x^2 + 4y^2 + 3z^2) - (4xy + 7y^2 - 3z^2 + 1)$$

$$= 5x^2 + 4y^2 + 3z^2 - 4xy - 7y^2 + 3z^2 - 1$$

$$= (5x^2) + (4y^2 - 7y^2) + (3z^2 + 3z^2) - 4xy - 1$$

$$= (5x^2) + (-3y^2) + (6z^2) - 4xy - 1$$

Multiplication of two or more monomials is achieved by using the laws of exponents, the rules of signs, and the commutative and associative laws of multiplication. For example,

$$(y^2) \, (5) \, (6y^2) \, (yz) \, (2z^2)$$

$$= (1) \, (5) \, (6) \, (1) \, (2) \, (y^2) \, (y^2) \, (yz) \, (z^2)$$

$$= (60) \, [(y^2) \, (y^2) \, (y)] \, [(z) \, (z^2)]$$

$$= 60(y^5) \, (z^3)$$

$$= 60y^5z^3$$

Multiplication of a polynomial by a monomial is achieved by multiplying each term of the polynomial by the monomials and combining the results. For example,

$$(4x^2 + 3y) \times (6xz^2) = 24x^3z^2 + 18xyz^2$$

Multiplication of a polynomial by a polynomial is achieved by multiplying each of the terms of one polynomial by each of the terms of the other polynomial and combining the result. For example,

$$(5y + z + 1) \times (y^2 + 2y)$$

$$= [(5y) \times (y^2) + (5y) \times (2y)] + [(z) \times (y^2) + (z) \times (2y)]$$

$$+ [(1) \times (y^2) + (1) \times (2y)]$$

$$= (5y^3 + 10y^2) + (y^2z + 2yz) + (y^2 + 2y)$$

$$= (5y^3) + (10y^2 + y^2) + (y^2z) + (2yz) + (2y)$$

$$= 5y^3 + 11y^2 + y^2z + 2yz + 2y$$

Division of a monomial by a monomial is achieved by finding the quotient of the constant coefficients and the quotients of the variable factors, followed by the multiplication of these quotients. For example,

$$6xyz^2 \div 2y^2z = (6/2)\,(x/1)\,(y/y^2)\,(z^2/z)$$

$$= 3xy^{-1}z$$

$$= 3xz/y$$

Division of a polynomial by a polynomial is achieved by following the given procedure called *long division*.

Step 1: The terms of both the polynomials are arranged in order of ascending or descending powers of one variable.

Step 2: The first term of the dividend is divided by the first term of the divisor which gives the first term of the quotient.

Step 3: The divisor is multiplied by the first term of the quotient and the result is subtracted from the dividend.

Step 4: Using the remainder obtained from step 3 as the new dividend, steps 2 and 3 are repeated until the remainder is zero or the degree of the remainder is less than the degree of the divisor.

Step 5: The result is written as follows:

$$\frac{\text{dividend}}{\text{divisor}} = \text{quotient} + \frac{\text{remainder}}{\text{divisor}}, \text{divisor} \neq 0$$

For example,

$$(2x^2 + x + 6) \div (x + 1)$$

$$
\require{enclose}
\begin{array}{r}
2x - 1 \\
x+1 \enclose{longdiv}{2x^2 + x + 6} \\
-(2x^2 + 2x) \\
\hline
-x + 6 \\
-(-x - 1) \\
\hline
7
\end{array}
$$

The result is

$$(2x^2 + x + 6) \div (x + 1) = 2x - 1 + \frac{7}{x+1}$$

Polynomial Factorization

To factor a polynomial completely is to find the prime factors of the polynomial with respect to a specified set of numbers, i.e., to express it as a product of polynomials whose coefficients are members of that set.

The following concepts are important while factoring polynomials.

The factors of an algebraic expression consist of two or more algebraic expressions which when multiplied together produce the given algebraic expression.

A prime factor is a polynomial with no factors other than itself and 1. The least common multiple for a set of numbers is the smallest quantity divisible by every number of the set. For algebraic expressions, the least common multiple is the polynomial of lowest degree and smallest numerical coefficients for which each of the given expressions will be a factor.

The greatest common factor for a set of numbers is the largest factor that is common to all members of the set.

For algebraic expressions, the greatest common factor is the polynomial of highest degree and largest numerical coefficients which is a factor of all the given expressions.

Some important formulae, useful for the factoring of polynomials, are listed below.

$$a(c + d) = ac + ad$$

$$(a + b)(a - b) = a^2 - b^2$$

$$(a + b)(a + b) = (a + b)^2 = a^2 + 2ab + b^2$$

$$(a - b)(a - b) = (a - b)^2 = a^2 - 2ab + b^2$$

$$(x + a)(x + b) = x^2 + (a + b)x + ab$$

$$(ax + b)(cx + d) = acx^2 + (ad + bc)x + bd$$

$$(a + b)(c + d) = ac + bc + ad + bd$$

$$(a + b)(a + b)(a + b) = (a + b)^3 = a^3 + 3a^2b + 3ab^2 + b^3$$

$$(a - b)(a - b)(a - b) = (a - b)^3 = a^3 - 3a^2b + 3ab^2 - b^3$$

$$(a - b)(a^2 + ab + b^2) = a^3 - b^3$$

$$(a + b)(a^2 - ab + b^2) = a^3 + b^3$$

$$(a + b + c)^2 = a^2 + b^2 + c^2 + 2ab + 2ac + 2bc$$

$$(a - b)(a^3 + a^2b + ab^2 + b^3) = a^4 - b^4$$

$$(a - b)(a^4 + a^3b + a^2b^2 + ab^3 + b^4) = a^5 - b^5$$

$$(a - b)(a^5 + a^4b + a^3b^2 + a^2b^3 + ab^4 + b^5) = a^6 - b^6$$

$$(a - b)(a^{n-1} + a^{n-2}b + a^{n-3}b^2 + \ldots + ab^{n-2} + b^{n-1}) = a^n - b^n$$

where n is any positive integer (1, 2, 3, 4, …).

$$(a + b)(a^{n-1} - a^{n-2}b + a^{n-3}b^2 - \ldots - ab^{n-2} + b^{n-1}) = a^n + b^n$$

where n is any positive odd integer (1, 3, 5, 7, …).

The procedure for factoring a polynomial completely is as follows:

Step 1: First find the greatest common factor if there is any. Then examine each factor remaining for greatest common factors.

Step 2: Continue factoring the factors obtained in step 1 until all factors other than monomial factors are prime. For example, factoring

$$4 - 16x^2,$$

$$4 - 16x^2 = 4(1 - 4x^2) = 4(1 + 2x)(1 - 2x)$$

Operations with Fractions and Rational Expressions

A *rational* expression is an algebraic expression which can be written as the quotient of two polynomials:

$$\frac{A}{B}, B \neq 0.$$

For example,

$$\frac{9}{4}, \frac{3x^2 + 5x}{y + 3}, \frac{9y}{10z}$$

To reduce a given fraction or a rational expression to its simplest form is to reduce the fraction or expression into an equivalent form such that its numerator and denominator have no common factor other than 1.

The operations performed on fractions are in a similar manner applicable to rational expressions.

A fraction that contains one or more fractions in either its numerator or denominator—or in both its numerator and denominator—is called a complex fraction. For example,

$$\frac{1}{\frac{x}{5}}, \quad \frac{\frac{1}{2}}{\frac{3}{y}}, \quad \frac{1+\frac{y}{x}}{1-\frac{4}{x^2+1}}$$

The procedure for simplifying complex fractions is as follows:

First, the terms in the numerator and denominator are separately combined. Then the combined term of the numerator is divided by the combined term of the denominator to obtain a simplified fraction. For example,

$$\frac{1-\dfrac{5}{x}+\dfrac{6}{x^2}}{1-\dfrac{6}{x}+\dfrac{8}{x^2}}$$

Combining the numerator, we get

$$1-\frac{5}{x}+\frac{6}{x^2}=\frac{x^2-5x+6}{x^2}$$
$$=\frac{(x-3)(x-2)}{x^2}$$

Combining the denominator, we get

$$1-\frac{6}{x}+\frac{8}{x^2}=\frac{x^2-6x+8}{x^2}$$
$$=\frac{(x-4)(x-2)}{x^2}$$

Dividing the resultant numerator by the resultant denominator, we get

$$\frac{\dfrac{(x-3)(x-2)}{x^2}}{\dfrac{(x-4)(x-2)}{x^2}} = \frac{(x-3)(x-2)}{x^2} \times \frac{x^2}{(x-4)(x-2)}$$

$$= \frac{x-3}{x-4}$$

EQUATIONS

Equations

An equation is defined as a statement of equality of two separate expressions known as members.

A conditional equation is an equation which is true for only certain values of the unknowns (variables) invoked. For example,

$y + 6 = 11$ is true for $y = 5$.

An equation which is true for all permissible values of the unknown in question is called an identity. For example,

$$2x = \frac{4}{2}x$$

is an identity of $x \in R$, i.e., it is true for all reals.

The values of the variables that satisfy a conditional equation are called solutions of the conditional equation; the set of all such values is known as the solution set.

The solution to an equation $f(x) = 0$ is called the root of the equation.

Equations with the same solutions are said to be equivalent equations.

A statement of equality between two expressions containing rational coefficients and whose exponents are integers is called a rational integral equation. The degree of the equation is given by the term with the highest power, as shown below:

$$a_n x^n + a_{n-1}x^{n-1} + a_{n-2}x^{n-2} + \ldots + a_1 x + a_0 = 0$$

where $a_n \neq 0$, the a_i, and $i = 1 \ldots n$ are rational constant coefficients and n is a positive integer.

Basic Laws of Equality

A) Replacing an expression of an equation by an equivalent expression results in an equation equivalent to the original one.

For example, given the equation below

$$3x + y + x + 2y = 15$$

We know that for the left side of this equation we can apply the commutative and distributive laws to get

$$3x + y + x + 2y = 4x + 3y$$

Since these are equivalent, we can replace the expression in the original equation with the simpler form to get

$$4x + 3y = 15$$

B) The addition or subtraction of the same expression on both sides of an equation results in an equivalent equation to the original one.

For example, given the equation

$$y + 6 = 10,$$

we can add (−6) to both sides

$$y + 6 + (-6) = 10 + (-6)$$

to get $y + 0 = 10 - 6 \Rightarrow y = 4.$

So $y + 6 = 10$ is equivalent to $y = 4.$

C) The multiplication or division on both sides of an equation by the same expression results in an equivalent equation to the original. For example,

$$3x = 6 \Rightarrow \frac{3x}{3} = \frac{6}{3} \Rightarrow x = 2$$

$3x = 6$ is equivalent to $x = 2.$

D) If both members of an equation are raised to the same power, then the resultant equation is equivalent to the original equation. For example,

$$a = x^2 y, (a)^2 = (x^2 y)^2, \text{ and } a^2 = x^4 y^2.$$

This applies for negative and fractional powers as well. For example,

$$x^2 = 3y^4.$$

If we raise both members to the –2 power, we get

$$\left(x^2\right)^{-2} = \left(3y^4\right)^{-2}$$

$$\frac{1}{\left(x^2\right)^2} = \frac{1}{\left(3y^4\right)}$$

$$\frac{1}{x^4} = \frac{1}{9y^8}$$

If we raise both members to the $^1/_2$ power, which is the same as taking the square root, we get

$$\left(x^2\right)^{\frac{1}{2}} = \left(3y^4\right)^{\frac{1}{2}}$$

$$x = \sqrt{3}y^2$$

E) The reciprocal of both members of an equation are equivalent to the original equation.

Note: The reciprocal of zero is undefined.

For example;

$$\frac{2x + y}{z} = \frac{5}{2}$$

$$\frac{z}{2x + y} = \frac{2}{5}$$

Equations with Absolute Values

When evaluating equations containing absolute values, proceed as follows:

$$|\,5 - 3x\,| = 7$$

is valid if either

$$5 - 3x = 7 \qquad \text{or} \qquad 5 - 3x = -7$$
$$-3x = 2 \qquad\qquad\qquad -3x = -12$$

$$x = \frac{-2}{3} \qquad\qquad\qquad x = 4$$

The solution set is therefore $x = (-^2/_3, 4)$.

LINEAR EQUATIONS AND SYSTEMS OF LINEAR EQUATIONS

Linear Equations

A linear equation in one variable is one that can be put into the form $ax + b = 0$, where a and b are constants, $a \neq 0$.

To solve a linear equation means to transform it in the form

$$x = \frac{-b}{a}.$$

A) If the equation has unknowns on both sides of the equality, it is convenient to put similar terms on the same side. For example,

$$4x + 3 = 2x + 9$$
$$4x + 3 - 2x = 2x + 9 - 2x$$
$$(4x - 2x) + 3 = (2x - 2x) + 9$$
$$2x + 3 = 0 + 9$$
$$2x + 3 - 3 = 0 + 9 - 3$$
$$2x = 6$$
$$\frac{2x}{2} = \frac{6}{2}$$
$$x = 3$$

B) If the equation appears in fractional form, it is necessary to transform it, using cross-multiplication, and then repeating the same procedure as in A), we obtain

$$\frac{3x + 4}{3} \diagdown\!\!\!\!\!\diagup \frac{7x + 2}{5}$$

By using cross-multiplication, we would obtain

$$3(7x + 2) = 5(3x + 4).$$

This is equivalent to

$$21x + 6 = 15x + 20$$

which can be solved as in A).

$$21x + 6 = 15x + 20$$
$$21x - 15x + 6 = 15x - 15x + 20$$

$$6x + 6 - 6 = 20 - 6$$

$$6x = 14$$

$$x = \frac{14}{6}$$

$$x = \frac{7}{3}$$

C) If there are radicals in the equation, it is necessary to square both sides and then apply A).

$$\sqrt{3x + 1} = 5$$

$$\left(\sqrt{3x + 1}\right)^2 = 5^2$$

$$3x + 1 = 25$$

$$3x + 1 - 1 = 25 - 1$$

$$3x = 24$$

$$x = \frac{24}{3}$$

$$x = 8$$

Linear Equations in Two Variables

Equations of the form $ax + by = c$, where a, b, and c are constants and $a, b \neq 0$ are called linear equations in two variables.

The solution set for a linear equation in two variables is the set of all x and y values for which the equation is true. An element in the solution set is called an ordered pair (x, y), where x and y are two of the values that together satisfy the equation. The x value is always first and is called the x-coordinate. The y value is always second and is called the y-coordinate.

Graphing the Solution Set

The solution set of the equation $ax + by = c$ can be represented by graphing the ordered pairs that satisfy the equation on a rectangular coordinate system. This is a system where two real number lines are drawn at right angles to each other. The point where the two lines intercept is called the origin and is associated to the ordered pair $(0, 0)$.

To plot a certain ordered pair (x, y), move x units along the x-axis in the direction indicated by the sign of x, then move y units along the y-axis in the direction indicated by the sign of y.

Note that movement to the right or up is positive, while movement to the left or down is negative.

EXAMPLE

Graph the following points: $(1, 2)$, $(-3, 2)$, $(-2, -1)$, $(1, -1)$.

To graph a linear equation in two variables, it is necessary to graph its solution set, that is, draw a line through the points whose coordinates satisfy the equation.

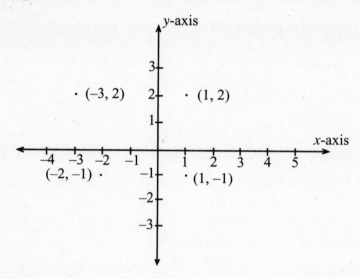

The resultant graph of a linear equation in two variables is a straight line.

There are several ways of graphing this line, two of them are shown below:

A) Plot 2 or more ordered pairs that satisfy the equation and then connect them.

B) Plot the points

$$A\left(\frac{c}{d}, 0\right) \text{ and } B\left(0, \frac{c}{b}\right)$$

that correspond to the point where the line intercepts the x-axis and y-axis, respectively, as shown:

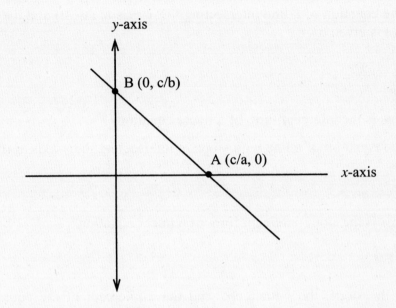

The slope of the line containing two points (x_1, y_1) and (x_2, y_2) is given by

$$\text{Slope} = m = \frac{y_2 - y_1}{x_2 - x_1}$$

Horizontal lines have a slope of zero, and the slope of vertical lines is undefined. Parallel lines have equal slopes, and perpendicular lines have slopes which are negative reciprocals.

The equation of a line with slope m passing through a point $Q(x_0, y_0)$ is of the form

$$y - y_0 = m(x - x_0).$$

This is called the point-slope form of a linear equation.

The equation of a line passing through $Q(x_1, y_1)$ and $P(x_2, y_2)$ is given by

$$\frac{x - x_1}{x_1 - x_2} = \frac{y - y_1}{y_1 - y_2}.$$

This is the two-point form of a linear equation.

The equation of a line intersecting the x-axis at $(x_0, 0)$ and the y-axis at $(0, y_0)$ is given by

$$\frac{x}{x_0} + \frac{y}{y_0} = 1.$$

This is the intercept form of a linear equation.

The equation of a line with slope m intersecting the y-axis at $(0, b)$ is given by

$$y = mx + b.$$

This is the slope-intercept form of a linear equation.

PROBLEM

Find the slope, the y-intercept, and the x-intercept of the equation $2x - 3y - 18 = 0$.

SOLUTION

The equation $2x - 3y - 18 = 0$ can be written in the form of the general linear equation, $ax + by = c$.

$$2x - 3y - 18 = 0$$

$$2x - 3y = 18$$

To find the slope and y-intercept, we derive them from the formula of the general linear equation $ax + by = c$. Dividing by b and solving for y we obtain

$$\frac{a}{b}x + y = \frac{c}{b}$$

$$y = \frac{c}{b} - \frac{a}{b}x$$

where $\dfrac{-a}{b}$ = slope and $\dfrac{c}{b}$ = y-intercept.

To find the x-intercept, solve for x and let $y = 0$:

$$x = \frac{c}{b} - \frac{b}{a} y$$

$$x = \frac{c}{a}$$

In this form we have $a = 2$, $b = -3$, and $c = 18$. Thus,

$$\text{slope} = -\frac{a}{b} = -\frac{2}{-3} = \frac{2}{3}$$

$$y\text{-intercept} = \frac{c}{b} = \frac{18}{-3} = -6$$

$$x\text{-intercept} = \frac{c}{a} = \frac{18}{2} = 9$$

PROBLEM

Find the equation for the line passing through $(3, 5)$ and $(-1, 2)$.

SOLUTION

Solution A

We use the two-point form with $(x_1, y_1) = (3, 5)$ and $(x_2, y_2) = (-1, 2)$. Then

$$\frac{y - y_1}{x - x_1} = m = \frac{y_2 - y_1}{x_2 - x_1}$$

$$\frac{y_2 - y_1}{x_2 - x_1} = \frac{2 - 5}{-1 - 3}$$

thus $\quad \dfrac{y - 5}{x - 3} = \dfrac{-3}{-4}$

Cross multiplying,

$$-4(y - 5) = -3(x - 3)$$

Distributing,

$$-4y + 20 = -3x + 9$$

$$3x - 4y = -11$$

Solution B

Does the same equation result if we let $(x_1, y_1) = (-1, 2)$ and $(x_2, y_2) = (3, 5)$?

$$\frac{y_2 - y_1}{x_2 - x_1} = \frac{5 - 2}{3 - (-1)}$$

thus $\quad \dfrac{y - 2}{x + 1} = \dfrac{3}{4}$

Cross multiplying,

$$4(y - 2) = 3(x + 1)$$

$$3x - 4y = -11$$

Hence, either replacement results in the same equation.

PROBLEM

(a) Find the equation of the line passing through (2, 5) with slope 3.

(b) Suppose a line passes through the y-axis at $(0, b)$. How can we write the equation if the point-slope form is used?

SOLUTION

(a)   In the point-slope form, let $x_1 = 2$, $y_1 = 5$, and $m = 3$. The point-slope form of a line is

$$y - y_1 = m(x - x_1)$$

$$y - 5 = 3(x - 2)$$

$$y - 5 = 3x - 6 \qquad \text{Distributive property}$$

$$y = 3x - 1 \qquad \text{Transposition}$$

(b) $y - b = m(x - 0)$

$$y = mx + b$$

PROBLEM

Graph the function defined by $3x - 4y = 12$.

SOLUTION

Solve for y:

$$3x - 4y = 12$$

$$-4y = 12 - 3x$$

$$y = -3 + \frac{3}{4}x$$

$$y = \frac{3}{4}x - 3$$

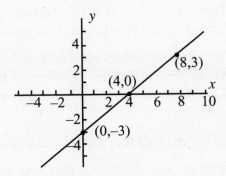

The graph of this function is a straight line since it is of the form $y = mx + b$. The y-intercept is the point $(0, -3)$ since for $x = 0$, $y = b = -3$. The x-intercept is the point $(4, 0)$ since for $y = 0$,

$$x = (y + 3) \times \frac{4}{3} = (0 + 3) \times \frac{4}{3} = 4.$$

These two points, $(0, -3)$ and $(4, 0)$, are sufficient to determine the graph (see the figure). A third point, $(8, 3)$, satisfying the equation of the function is plotted as a partial check of the intercepts. Note that the slope of the line is $m = \frac{3}{4}$. This means that y increases 3 units as x increases 4 units anywhere along the line.

Systems of Linear Equations

A system of linear equations is a set of one or more linear equations as shown below.

$$\begin{cases} 2x + 4y = 11 \\ -5x + 3y = 5 \end{cases}$$

The set shown above is a system of linear equations with two variables, or unknowns.

There are several ways to solve systems of linear equations in two variables:

Method 1: **Addition or subtraction**—if necessary multiply the equations by numbers that will make the coefficients of one unknown in the resulting equations numerically equal. If the signs of equal coefficients are the same, subtract the equation, otherwise add.

The result is one equation with one unknown; we solve it and substitute the value into the other equations to find the unknown that we first eliminated.

Method 2: **Substitution**—find the value of one unknown in terms of the other; substitute this value in the other equation and solve.

Method 3: **Graph**—graph both equations. The point of intersection of the drawn lines is a simultaneous solution for the equations and its coordinates correspond to the answer that would be found analytically.

If the lines are parallel they have no simultaneous solution.

Dependent equations are equations that represent the same line; therefore, every point on the line of a dependent equation represents a solution. Since there is an infinite number of points, there is an infinite number of simultaneous solutions, for example:

$$\begin{cases} 2x + y = 8 \\ 4x + 2y = 16 \end{cases}$$

The equations above are dependent; they represent the same line. All points that satisfy either of the equations are solutions of the system.

A system of linear equations is consistent if there is only one solution for the system.

A system of linear equations is inconsistent if it does not have any solutions.

PROBLEM

Find the point of intersection of the graphs of the equations:

$$\begin{cases} x + y = 3 \\ 3x - 3y = 14 \end{cases}$$

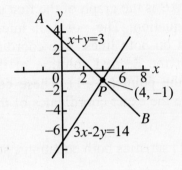

SOLUTION

To solve these linear equations, solve for y in terms of x. The equations will be in the form $y = mx + b$, where m is the slope and b is the intercept on the y-axis.

$$x + y = 3$$

$$y = 3 - x \qquad \text{Subtract } x \text{ from both sides.}$$

$$3x - 2y = 14 \qquad \text{Subtract } 3x \text{ from both sides.}$$

$$-2y = 14 - 3x \qquad \text{Divide by } -2.$$

$$y = -7 + \frac{3}{2}x$$

The graphs of the linear functions, $y = 3 - x$ and $y = -7 + {}^{3}/{}_{2}x$, can be determined by plotting only two points. For example, for $y = 3 - x$, let $x = 0$, then $y = 3$. Let $x = 1$, then $y = 2$. The two points on this first line are $(0, 3)$ and $(1, 2)$. For $y = -7 + {}^{3}/{}_{2}x$, let $x = 0$, then $y = -7$. Let $x = 1$, then $y = -5{}^{1}/{}_{2}$. The two points on this second line are $(0, -7)$ and $(1, -5{}^{1}/{}_{2})$.

To find the point of intersection P of

$$x + y = 3$$

and $\qquad 3x - 2y = 14,$

solve them algebraically. Multiply the first equation by 2. Add these two equations to eliminate the variable y.

$$
\begin{aligned}
2x + 2y &= 6 \\
3x - 2y &= 14 \\
\hline
5x &= 20
\end{aligned}
$$

Solve for x to obtain $x = 4$. Substitute this into $y = 3 - x$ to get $y = 3 - 4 = -1$. P is $(4, -1)$. AB is the graph of the first equation, and CD is the graph of the second equation. The point of intersection P of the two graphs is the only point on both lines. The coordinates of P satisfy both equations and represent the desired solution of the problem. From the graph, P seems to be the point $(4, -1)$. These coordinates satisfy both equations, and hence are the exact coordinates of the point of intersection of the two lines.

To show that $(4, -1)$ satisfies both equations, substitute this point into both equations.

$$x + y = 3 \qquad\qquad 3x - 2y = 14$$
$$4 + (-1) = 3 \qquad\qquad 3(4) - 2(-1) = 14$$
$$4 - 1 = 3 \qquad\qquad 12 + 2 = 14$$
$$3 = 3 \qquad\qquad 14 = 14$$

PROBLEM

Solve the equations $2x + 3y = 6$ and $4x + 6y = 7$ simultaneously.

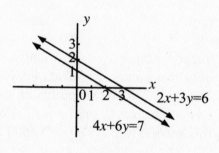

SOLUTION

We have two equations and two unknowns,

$$2x + 3y = 6 \tag{1}$$

and $\quad 4x + 6y = 7 \tag{2}$

There are several methods to solve this problem. We have chosen to multiply each equation by a different number so that when the two equations are added, one of the variables drops out. Thus, multiplying equation

(1) by 2:

$$4x + 6y = 12 \tag{3}$$

multiplying equation (2) by –1:

$$-4x - 6y = -7 \tag{4}$$

adding equations (3) and (4):

$$0 = 5$$

We obtain a peculiar result!

Actually, what we have shown in this case is that if there were a simultaneous solution to the given equations, then 0 would equal 5. But the conclusion is impossible; therefore, there can be no simultaneous solution to these two equations, hence no point satisfying both.

The straight lines which are the graphs of these equations must be parallel if they never intersect, but not identical, which can be seen from the graph of these equations (see the accompanying diagram).

PROBLEM

Solve the equations $2x + 3y = 6$ and $y = -(2x/3) + 2$ simultaneously.

SOLUTION

We have two equations and two unknowns,

$$2x + 3y = 6 \tag{1}$$

$$y = \frac{2x}{3} + 2 \tag{2}$$

There are several methods of solution for this problem. Since equation (2) already gives us an expression for y, we use the method of substitution. Substituting $-(2x/3) + 2$ for y in the first equation:

$$2x + 3\left(-\frac{2x}{3} + 2\right) = 6$$

Distributing, $\qquad 2x - 2x + 6 = 6$

$$6 = 6$$

Apparently we have gotten nowhere! The result $6 = 6$ is true, but indicates no solution. Actually, our work shows that no matter what real number x

is, if y is determined by the second equation, then the first equation will always be satisfied.

The reason for this peculiarity may be seen if we take a closer look at the equation $y = -(2x/3) + 2$. It is equivalent to $3y = -2x + 6$, or $2x + 3y = 6$.

In other words, the two equations are equivalent. Any pair of values of x and y which satisfies one satisfies the other.

It is hardly necessary to verify that in this case the graphs of the given equations are identical lines, and that there are an infinite number of simultaneous solutions of these equations.

A system of three linear equations in three unknowns is solved by eliminating one unknown from any two of the three equations and solving them. After finding two unknowns, substitute them in any of the equations to find the third unknown.

PROBLEM

Solve the system

$$2x + 3y - 4z = -8 \tag{1}$$

$$x + y - 2z = -5 \tag{2}$$

$$7x - 2y + 5z = 4 \tag{3}$$

SOLUTION

We cannot eliminate any variable from two pairs of equations by a single multiplication. However, both x and z may be eliminated from equations (1) and (2) by multiplying equation (2) by -2. Then

$$2x + 3y - 4z = -8 \tag{1}$$

$$-2x - 2y + 4z = 10 \tag{4}$$

By addition, we have $y = 2$. Although we may now eliminate either x or z from another pair of equations, we can more conveniently substitute $y = 2$ in equations (2) and (3) to get two equations in two variables. Thus, making the substitution $y = 2$ in equations (2) and (3), we have

$$x - 2z = -7 \tag{5}$$

$$7x + 5z = 8 \tag{6}$$

Multiply equation (5) by 5 and multiply (6) by 2, then add the two new equations. We get $x = -1$. Substitute x in either (5) or (6) to find z.

The solution of the system is $x = -1$, $y = 2$, and $z = 3$. Check by substitution.

A system of equations, as shown below, that has all constant terms $b_1, b_2, \ldots b_n$ equal to zero is said to be a homogeneous system:

$$\begin{cases} a_{11}x_1 + a_{12}x_2 + \ldots + a_{1n}x_m = b_1 \\ a_{21}x_1 + a_{22}x_2 + \ldots + a_{2n}x_m = b_2 \\ \vdots \qquad \vdots \qquad\quad \vdots \qquad \vdots \\ a_{n1}x_1 + a_{n2}x_2 + \ldots + a_{nn}x_m = b_n \end{cases}$$

A homogeneous system always has at least one solution which is called the trivial solution that is $x_1 = 0$, $x_2 = 0, \ldots, x_m = 0$.

For any given homogeneous system of equations, in which the number of variables is greater than or equal to the number of equations, there are non-trivial solutions.

Two systems of linear equations are said to be equivalent if and only if they have the same solution set.

INEQUALITIES

Inequality

An inequality is a statement that the value of one quantity or expression is greater than or less than that of another.

EXAMPLE

$5 > 4$

The expression above means that the value of 5 is greater than the value of 4.

A conditional inequality is an inequality whose validity depends on the values of the variables in the sentence. That is, certain values of the variables will make the sentence true, and others will make it false. $3 - y > 3 + y$ is a conditional inequality for the set of real numbers, since it is true for any replacement less than zero and false for all others.

$x + 5 > x + 2$ is an absolute inequality for the set of real numbers, meaning that for any real value x, the expression on the left is greater than the expression on the right.

$5x < 2x + x$ is inconsistent for the set of non-negative real numbers. For any x greater than 0, the sentence is always false. A sentence is inconsistent if it is always false when its variables assume allowable values.

The solution of a given inequality in one variable x consists of all values of x for which the inequality is true.

The graph of an inequality in one variable is represented by either a ray or a line segment on the real number line.

The endpoint is not a solution if the variable is strictly less than or greater than a particular value.

EXAMPLE

$x > 2$

$x > 2$

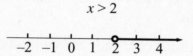

2 is not a solution and should be represented as shown.

The endpoint is a solution if the variable is either 1) less than or equal to or 2) greater than or equal to a particular value.

EXAMPLE

$5 > x \geq 2$

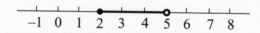

In this case 2 is the solution and should be represented as shown.

Properties of Inequalities

If x and y are real numbers, then one and only one of the following statements is true.

$x > y, x = y,$ or $x < y.$

This is the order property of real numbers.

If $a, b,$ and c are real numbers:

A)   If $a < b$ and $b < c$, then $a < c$.

B)   If $a > b$ and $b > c$, then $a > c$.

This is the transitive property of inequalities.

If a, b, and c are real numbers and $a > b$, then $a + c > b + c$ and $a - c > b - c$. This is the addition property of inequalities.

Two inequalities are said to have the same sense if their signs of inequality point in the same direction.

The sense of an inequality remains the same if both sides are multiplied or divided by the same positive real number. For example,

   $4 > 3$

If we multiply both sides by 5, we will obtain

   $4 \times 5 > 3 \times 5$

   $20 > 15$

The sense of the inequality does not change.

The sense of an inequality becomes opposite if each side is multiplied or divided by the same negative real number. For example,

   $4 > 3$

If we multiply both sides by -5, we would obtain

   $4 \times -5 < 3 \times -5$

   $-20 < -15$

The sense of the inequality becomes opposite.

If $a > b$ and a, b, and n are positive real numbers, then,

   $a^n > b^n$ and $a^{-n} < b^{-n}$.

If $x > y$ and $q > p$, then $x + q > y + p$.

If $x > y > 0$ and $q > p > 0$, then $xq > yp$.

Inequalities that have the same solution set are called equivalent inequalities.

Inequalities with Absolute Values

The solution set of $|x| < a$, $a > 0$, is $\{x \mid -a < x < a\}$.

The solution set of $|x| > a$ is $\{x \mid x > a \text{ or } x < -a\}$.

Inequalities in Two Variables

An inequality of the form $ax + by < c$ is a linear inequality in two variables. The equation for the boundary of the solution set is given by $ax + by = c$.

To graph a linear inequality, first graph the boundary.

Next, choose any point off the boundary and substitute its coordinates into the original inequality. If the resulting statement is true, the graph lies on the same side of the boundary as the test point. A false statement indicates that the solution set lies on the other side of the boundary.

PROBLEM

Solve $2x - 3y \geq 6$.

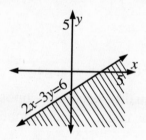

SOLUTION

The statement $2x - 3y \geq 6$ means $2x - 3y$ is greater than or equal to 6. Symbolically, we have $2x - 3y > 6$ or $2x - 3y = 6$. Consider the corresponding equality and graph $2x - 3y = 6$. To find the x-intercept, set $y = 0$.

$$2x - 3y = 6$$
$$2x - 3(0) = 6$$
$$2x = 6$$
$$x = 3$$

$\{3, 0\}$ is the x-intercept.

To find the y-intercept, set $x = 0$.

$$2x - 3y = 6$$
$$2(0) - 3y = 6$$
$$-3y = 6$$
$$y = -2$$

$\{0, -2\}$ is the y-intercept.

A line is determined by two points. Therefore, draw a straight line through the two intercepts {3, 0} and {0, –2}. Since the inequality is mixed, a solid line is drawn through the intercepts. This line represents the part of the statement $2x - 3y = 6$.

We must now determine the region for which the inequality $2x - 3y > 6$ holds.

Choose two points to decide on which side of the line the region $2x - 3y > 6$ lies. We shall try the points $(0, 0)$ and $(5, 1)$.

For (0, 0)	For (5, 1)
$2x - 3y > 6$	$2x - 3y > 6$
$2(0) - 3(0) > 6$	$2(5) - 3(1) > 6$
$0 - 0 > 6$	$10 - 3 > 6$
$0 > 6$	$7 > 6$
False	True

The inequality, $2x - 3y > 6$, holds true for the point $(5, 1)$. We shade this region of the xy-plane. That is, the area lying below the line $2x - 3y = 6$ and containing $(5, 1)$.

Therefore, the solution contains the solid line, $2x - 3y = 6$, and the part of the plane below this line for which the statement $2x - 3y > 6$ holds.

Systems of Linear Inequalities

To graph a system of linear inequalities, graph each inequality individually on the same graph, using different types of shading to indicate each one. The intersection of all the shaded areas is the area on which the inequality is valid.

PROBLEM

> Solve.
>
> $2x - 3y \geq 6$
>
> $y \geq 0$
>
> $5x + y < 2$

SOLUTION

First, superimpose the graphs of the three inequalities:

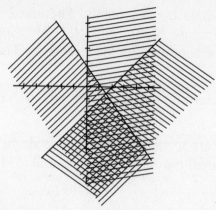

The area of intersection is:

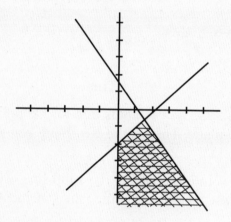

RELATIONS AND FUNCTIONS

Relations and Functions

A relation is any set of ordered pairs. The set of all first members of the ordered pairs is called the domain of the relation and the set of all second members of the ordered pairs is called the range of the relation.

PROBLEM

Find the relation defined by $y^2 = 25 - x^2$ where the domain $D = \{0, 3, 4, 5\}$.

SOLUTION

x takes on the values 0, 3, 4, and 5. Replacing x by these values in the equation $y^2 = 25 - x^2$, we obtain the corresponding values of y (see Table 8.1).

Hence the relation defined by $y^2 = 25 - x^2$ where x belongs to $D = \{0, 3, 4, 5\}$ is

$$\{(0, 5), (0, -5), (3, 4), (3, -4), (4, 3), (4, -3), (5, 0)\}.$$

The domain of the relation is $(0, 3, 4, 5)$. The range of the relation is $(5, -5, 4, -4, 3, -3, 0)$.

A function is a relation in which no two ordered pairs have the same first member. For example,

$$X = \{1, 2, 3, 4, 5, 6, 7, 8\} \text{ and } Y = \{2, 4, 6, 8\}$$

A function with domain X and range Y could be given by:

x	$y^2 = 25 - x^2$	y
0	$y^2 = 25 - 0$ $y^2 = 25$ $y = \sqrt{25}$ $y = \pm 5$	± 5
3	$y^2 = 25 - 3^2$ $y^2 = 25 - 9$ $y^2 = 16$ $y = \sqrt{16}$ $y = \pm 4$	± 4
4	$y^2 = 25 - 4^2$ $y^2 = 25 - 16$ $y^2 = 9$ $y = \sqrt{9}$ $y = \pm 3$	± 3
5	$y^2 = 25 - 5^2$ $y^2 = 25 - 25$ $y^2 = 0$ $y = 0$	0

$$\{(1, 2), (2, 2), (3, 4), (4, 4), (5, 6), (6, 6), (7, 8), (8, 8)\}$$

You can see above that every member of the domain is paired with one and only one member of the range. Then this relation is called a function and is represented by $y = f(x)$, where $x \, \varepsilon \, X$ and $y \, \varepsilon \, Y$. If f is a function that takes an element $x \, \varepsilon \, X$ and sends it to an element $y \, \varepsilon \, Y$, f is said to map x into y. We write this as $f{:}x{\to}y$. For this reason, a function is also called a mapping.

Given $f{:}x{\to}y$, we can also say that y is a function of x, denoted $f(x) = y$, "f of x equals y." In this function, y is called the dependent variable, since it derives its value from x. By the same reasoning, x is called the independent variable.

Another way of checking if a relation is a function is the vertical line test: if there does not exist any vertical line which crosses the graph of a relation in more than one place, then the relation is a function. If the domain of a relation or a function is not specified, it is assumed to be all real numbers.

Properties of Relations

A relation R from set A to set B is a subset of the Cartesian Product $A \times B$ written aRb with $a \, \varepsilon \, A$ and $b \, \varepsilon \, B$.

Let R be a relation from a set S to itself. Then

A) R is said to be reflexive if and only if sRs for every $s \, \varepsilon \, S$.

B) R is said to be symmetric if $s_iRs_j \Rightarrow s_jRs_i$ where $s_i, s_j \, \varepsilon \, S$.

C) R is said to be transitive if s_iRs_j and s_jRs_k implies s_iRs_k.

D) R is said to be anti-symmetric if s_1Rs_2 and s_2Rs_1 implies $s_1 = s_2$.

A relation R on $S \times S$ is called an equivalence relation if R is reflexive, symmetric, and transitive.

Properties of Functions

If f and g are two functions with a common domain, then the sum of f and g, written $f + g$, is defined by

$$(f + g)\,(x) = f(x) + g(x).$$

The difference of f and g is defined by

$$(f - g)\,(x) = f(x) - g(x).$$

The quotient of f and g is defined by

$$\left(\frac{f}{g}\right)(x) = \frac{f(x)}{g(x)}, \text{ where } g\,(x) \neq 0.$$

PROBLEM

Let $f(x) = 2x^2$ with domain $D_f = R$ and $g(x) = x - 5$ with $D_g = R$. Find

   (a) $f + g$ (c) fg

   (b) $f - g$ (d) $\dfrac{f}{g}$

SOLUTION

(a) $f + g$ has domain R and

$$(f + g)(x) = f(x) + g(x) = 2x^2 + x - 5$$

for each number x. For example,

$$(f + g)(1) = f(1) + g(1) = 2(1)^2 + 1 - 5 = 2 - 4 = -2$$

(b) $f - g$ has domain R and

$$(f - g)(x) = f(x) - g(x) = 2x^2 - (x - 5) = 2x^2 - x + 5$$

for each number x. For example,

$$(f - g)(1) = f(1) - g(1) = 2(1)^2 - 1 + 5 = 2 + 4 = 6$$

(c) fg has domain R and

$$(fg)(x) = f(x) \times g(x) = 2x^2 \times (x - 5) = 2x^3 - 10x^2$$

for each number x. In particular,

$$(fg)(1) = 2(1)^3 - 10(1)^2 = 2 - 10 = -8$$

(d) $\dfrac{f}{g}$ has domain R excluding the number $x = 5$ (when $x = 5$, $g(x) = 0$ and division by zero is undefined) and

$$\left(\frac{f}{g}\right)(x) = \frac{f(x)}{g(x)} = \frac{2x^2}{x - 5}$$

for each number $x \neq 5$. In particular,

$$\left(\frac{f}{g}\right)(1) = \frac{2(1)^2}{1 - 5} = \frac{2}{-4} = -\frac{1}{2}$$

If f is a function, the inverse of f, written f^{-1}, is such that:

$$(x, y) \,\varepsilon\, f \Leftrightarrow (y, x) \,\varepsilon\, f^{-1}$$

The graph of f^{-1} can be obtained from the graph of f by simply reflecting the graph of f across the line $y = x$. The graphs of f and f^{-1} are symmetrical about the line $y = x$.

The inverse of a function is not necessarily a function.

PROBLEM

Show that the inverse of the function $y = x^2 + 4x - 5$ is not a function.

SOLUTION

Given the function f such that no two of its ordered pairs have the same second element, the inverse function f^{-1} is the set of ordered pairs obtained from f by interchanging in each ordered pair the first and second elements. Thus, the inverse of the function

$$y = x^2 + 4x - 5 \text{ is } x = y^2 + 4y - 5.$$

The given function has more than one first component corresponding to a given second component. For example, if $y = 0$, then $x = -5$ or 1. If the elements $(-5, 0)$ and $(1, 0)$ are reversed, we have $(0, -5)$ and $(0, 1)$ as elements of the inverse. Since the first component 0 has more than one second component, the inverse is not a function (a function can have only one y value corresponding to each x value).

A function $f : A \rightarrow B$ is said to be one-to-one or injective if distinct elements in the domain A have distinct images, i.e., if $f(x) = f(y)$ implies $x = y$. For an example: $y = f(x) = x^2$ defined over the domain $\{x \,\varepsilon\, R \mid x \geq 0\}$ is an injection or an injective function.

A function $f : A \rightarrow B$ is said to be a surjective or an onto function if each element of B is the image of some element of A, i.e., $f(A) = B$. For instance, $y = x^3 \sin x$ is a surjection or a surjective function.

A function $f : A \rightarrow B$ is said to be bijective or a bijective if f is both injective and surjective. f is also called a one-to-one correspondence between A and B. An example of such a function would be $y = x$.

QUADRATIC EQUATIONS

Quadratic Equation

A second degree equation in x of the type $ax^2 + bx + c = 0$, where $a \neq 0$, a, b, and c are real numbers, is called a quadratic equation.

To solve a quadratic equation is to find values of x which satisfy $ax^2 + bx + c = 0$. These values of x are called solutions, or roots, of the equation.

A quadratic equation has a maximum of two roots. Methods of solving quadratic equations:

A) **Direct Solution**: Given $x^2 - 9 = 0$.

    We can solve directly by isolating the variable x.

    $$x^2 = 9$$

    $$x = \pm 3$$

B) **Factoring:** Given a quadratic equation $ax^2 + bx + c = 0$, $a, b, c \neq 0$, to factor means to express it as the product $a(x - r_1)(x - r_2) = 0$, where r_1 and r_2 are the two roots.

    Some helpful hints to remember are:

    a) $$r_1 + r_2 = -\frac{b}{a}$$

    b) $$r_1 r_2 = \frac{c}{a}$$

    Given $x^2 - 5x + 4 = 0$.

    Since

    $$r_1 + r_2 = \frac{-b}{a} = \frac{-(-5)}{1} = 5,$$

    the possible solutions are $(3, 2)$, $(4, 1)$, and $(5, 0)$. Also,

    $$r_1 r_2 = \frac{c}{a} = \frac{4}{1} = 4;$$

    this equation is satisfied only by the second pair, so $r_1 = 4$, $r_2 = 1$, and the factored form is $(x - 4)(x - 1) = 0$.

    If the coefficient of x^2 is not 1, it may be easier to divide the equation by this coefficient and then factor.

    Given $2x^2 - 12x + 16 = 0$

    Dividing by 2, we obtain:

    $$x^2 - 6x + 8 = 0$$

Since

$$r_1 + r_2 = \frac{-b}{a} = 6,$$

the possible solutions are (6, 0), (5, 1), (4, 2), and (3, 3). Also $r_1 r_2 = 8$, so the only possible answer is (4, 2) and the expression $x^2 - 6x + 8 = 0$ can be factored as $(x - 4)(x - 2)$.

C) **Completing the Squares:** If it is difficult to factor the quadratic equation using the previous method, we can complete the squares.

Given $x^2 - 12x + 8 = 0$

We know that the sum of the two roots should be 12 because

$$r_1 + r_2 = \frac{-b}{a} = \frac{-(-12)}{1} = 12.$$

The possible roots are (12, 0), (11, 1), (10, 2), (9, 3), (8, 4), (7, 5), and (6, 6).

But none of these satisfy $r_1 r_2 = 8$, so we cannot use method (B), factoring.

To complete the square, it is necessary to isolate the constant term,

$$x^2 - 12x = -8.$$

Then take $^1/_2$ coefficient of x, square it, and add to both sides.

$$x^2 - 12x + \left(\frac{-12}{2}\right)^2 = -8 + \left(\frac{-12}{2}\right)^2$$

$$x^2 - 12x + 36 = -8 + 36 = 28$$

Now we can use the previous method to factor the left side:

$$r_1 + r_2 = 12, \, r_1 r_2 = 36$$

is satisfied by the pair (6, 6), so we have

$$(x - 6)^2 = 28.$$

Now extract the root of both sides and solve for x.

$$(x - 6) = \pm\sqrt{28} = \pm 2\sqrt{7}$$
$$x = \pm 2\sqrt{7} + 6$$

So the roots are: $x = 2\sqrt{7} + 6$, $x = -2\sqrt{7} + 6$.

Quadratic Formula

Consider the polynomial:

$ax^2 + bx + c = 0$, where $a \neq 0$.

The roots of this equation can be determined in terms of the coefficients a, b, and c as shown below:

$$x = \frac{-b \pm \sqrt{b^2 - 4ac}}{2a}$$

where $(b^2 - 4ac)$ is called the discriminant of the quadratic equation.

Note that if the discriminant is less than zero $(b^2 - 4ax < 0)$, the roots are complex numbers, since the discriminant appears under a radical and square roots of negatives are complex numbers, and a real number added to an imaginary number yields a complex number.

If the discriminant is equal to zero $(b^2 - 4ac = 0)$, the roots are real and equal.

If the discriminant is greater than zero $(b^2 - 4ac > 0)$, then the roots are real and unequal. Further, the roots are rational if and only if a and b are rational and $(b^2 - 4ac)$ is a perfect square, otherwise the roots are irrational.

For example, compute the value of the discriminant and then determine the nature of the roots of each of the following four equations:

$4x^2 - 12x + 9 = 0$,

$3x^2 - 7x - 6 = 0$,

$5x^2 + 2x - 9 = 0$,

and $x^2 + 3x + 5 = 0$.

A) $4x^2 - 12x + 9 = 0$,

Here, a, b, and c are integers:

$a = 4$, $b = -12$, and $c = 9$.

Therefore,

$b^2 - 4ac = (-12)^2 - 4(4)(9) = 144 - 144 = 0$

Since the discriminant is 0, the roots are rational and equal.

B) $3x^2 - 7x - 6 = 0$

Here, a, b, and c are integers:

$a = 3$, $b = -7$, and $c = -6$.

Therefore,

$b^2 - 4ac = (-7)^2 - 4(3)(-6) = 49 + 72 = 121 = 11^2$.

Since the discriminant is a perfect square, the roots are rational and unequal.

C) $5x^2 + 2x - 9 = 0$

Here, a, b, and c are integers:

$a = 5$, $b = 2$, and $c = -9$

Therefore,

$b^2 - 4ac = 2^2 - 4(5)(-9) = 4 + 180 = 184$.

Since the discriminant is greater than zero, but not a perfect square, the roots are irrational and unequal.

D) $x^2 + 3x + 5 = 0$

Here, a, b, and c are integers:

$a = 1$, $b = 3$, and $c = 5$

Therefore,

$b^2 - 4ac = 3^2 - 4(1)(5) = 9 - 20 = -11$

Since the discriminant is negative, the roots are imaginary.

PROBLEM

Find the equation whose roots are $\dfrac{\alpha}{\beta}$, $\dfrac{\beta}{\alpha}$.

SOLUTION

The roots of the equation are (1) $x = \dfrac{\alpha}{\beta}$ and (2) $x = \dfrac{\beta}{\alpha}$. Subtract $\dfrac{\alpha}{\beta}$ from both sides of the first equation:

$$x - \frac{\alpha}{\beta} = \frac{\alpha}{\beta} - \frac{\alpha}{\beta} = 0,$$

or $\quad x - \dfrac{\alpha}{\beta} = 0.$

Subtract $\dfrac{\beta}{\alpha}$ from both sides of the second equation:

$$x - \frac{\beta}{\alpha} = \frac{\beta}{\alpha} - \frac{\beta}{\alpha} = 0,$$

or $\quad x - \dfrac{\beta}{\alpha} = 0.$

Therefore:

$$\left(x - \frac{\alpha}{\beta} \right)\left(x - \frac{\beta}{\alpha} \right) = (0)\,(0),$$

or $\quad \left(x - \dfrac{\alpha}{\beta} \right)\left(x - \dfrac{\beta}{\alpha} \right) = 0.$ $\hspace{2cm}$ (1)

Equation (1) is of the form:

$$(x - c)\,(x - d) = 0,$$

or $\quad x^2 - cx - dx + cd = 0,$

or $\quad x^2 - (c + d)x + cd = 0.$ $\hspace{2cm}$ (2)

Note that c corresponds to the root $\dfrac{\alpha}{\beta}$ and d corresponds to the root $\dfrac{\beta}{\alpha}$. The sum of the roots is

$$c + d = \frac{\alpha}{\beta} + \frac{\beta}{\alpha} = \frac{\alpha(\alpha)}{\alpha(\beta)} + \frac{\beta(\beta)}{\beta(\alpha)} = \frac{\alpha^2}{\alpha\beta} + \frac{\beta^2}{\alpha\beta} = \frac{\alpha^2 + \beta^2}{\alpha\beta}.$$

The product of the roots is

$$c \times d = \frac{\alpha}{\beta} \times \frac{\beta}{\alpha} = \frac{\alpha\beta}{\beta\alpha} = \frac{\alpha\beta}{\alpha\beta} = 1.$$

Using the form of equation (2):

$$\left(x - \frac{\alpha}{\beta}\right)\left(x - \frac{\beta}{\alpha}\right) = x^2 - \left(\frac{\alpha^2 + \beta^2}{\alpha\beta}\right)x + 1 = 0.$$

Hence,

$$x^2 - \left(\frac{\alpha^2 + \beta^2}{\alpha\beta}\right)x + 1 = 0. \tag{3}$$

Multiply both sides of equation (3) by $\alpha\beta$:

$$\alpha\beta\left[x^2 - \left(\frac{\alpha^2 + \beta^2}{\alpha\beta}\right)x + 1\right] = \alpha\beta(0)$$

Distributing,

$$\alpha\beta x^2 - (\alpha^2 + \beta^2)x + \alpha\beta = 0,$$

which is the equation whose roots are $\dfrac{\alpha}{\beta}, \dfrac{\beta}{\alpha}$.

Radical Equation

An equation that has one or more unknowns under a radical is called a radical equation.

To solve a radical equation, isolate the radical term on one side of the equation and move all the other terms to the other side. Then both members of the equation are raised to a power equal to the index of the isolated radical.

After solving the resulting equation, the roots obtained must be checked, since this method often introduces extraneous roots.

These introduced roots must be excluded if they are not solutions.

Given

$$\sqrt{x^2 + 2} + 6x = x - 4$$

$$\sqrt{x^2 + 2} = x - 4 - 6x = -5x - 4$$

$$\left(\sqrt{x^2 + 2}\right)^2 = (-(5x + 4))^2$$

$$x^2 + 2 = (5x + 4)^2$$

$$x^2 + 2 = 25x^2 + 40x + 16$$

$$24x^2 + 40x + 14 = 0.$$

Applying the quadratic formula, we obtain:

$$x = \frac{-40 \pm \sqrt{1,600 - 4(24)(14)}}{2(24)} = \frac{-40 \pm 16}{48}$$

$$x_1 = \frac{-7}{6}, \; x_2 = \frac{-1}{2}$$

Checking roots:

$$\sqrt{\left(\frac{-7}{6}\right)^2 + 2} + 6\left(\frac{-7}{6}\right) \overset{?}{=} \left(-\frac{7}{6}\right) - 4$$

$$\frac{11}{6} - 7 \overset{?}{=} \frac{-31}{6}$$

$$\frac{-31}{6} = \frac{-31}{6}$$

$$\sqrt{\left(\frac{-1}{2}\right)^2 + 2} + 6\left(\frac{-1}{2}\right) \overset{?}{=} \left(\frac{-1}{2}\right) - 4$$

$$\frac{3}{2} - 3 \overset{?}{=} \frac{-9}{2}$$

$$\frac{-3}{2} \neq \frac{-9}{2}$$

Hence, $-1/2$ is not a root of the equation.

Quadratic Functions

The function $f(x) = ax^2 + bx + c$, $a \neq 0$ where a, b, and c are real numbers, is called a quadratic function (or a function of second degree) in one unknown.

The graph of $y = ax^2 + bx + c$ is a curve known as a parabola.

The vertex of the parabola is the point.

$$v\left(\frac{-b}{2a}, \frac{4ac - b^2}{4a}\right).$$

The parabola's axis is the line

$$x = \frac{-b}{2a}.$$

The graph of the parabola opens upward if $a > 0$ and downward if $a < 0$. If $a = 0$ the quadratic function is reduced to a linear function whose graph is a straight line.

The figures below show parabolas with $a > 0$ and $a < 0$, respectively.

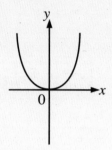

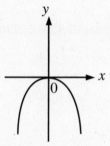

Quadratic Equations and Two Unknowns

A quadratic equation and two unknowns has the general form:

$$ax^2 + bxy + cy^2 + dx + ey + f = 0$$

where a, b, and c are not all zero and a, b, c, d, e, and f are constants.

Graphing: If $b^2 - 4ac < 0$, $b \neq 0$ and $a \neq c$, the graph of

$$ax^2 + bxy + cy^2 + dx + ey + f$$

is a closed curve called an ellipse. If $b = 0$ and $a = c$, the graph of

$$ax^2 + bxy + cy^2 + dx + ey + f$$

is a point or a circle, or else it does not exist.

If $b^2 - 4ac > 0$, the graph of

$$ax^2 + bxy + cy^2 + dx + ey + f = 0$$

is a curve called a hyperbola or two intersecting lines.

If $b^2 - 4ac = 0$, the graph of

$$ax^2 + bxy + cy^2 + dx + ey + f = 0$$

is a parabola or a pair of parallel lines which may be coincident, else it does not exist.

Solving Systems of Equations Involving Quadratics

Some methods for solving systems of equations involving quadratics are given below:

A) **One linear and one quadratic equation**

Solve the linear equation for one of the two unknowns, then substitute this value into the quadratic equation.

B) **Two quadratic equations**

Eliminate one of the unknowns using the method given for solving systems of linear equations.

For example,

$$x^2 + y^2 = 9 \qquad (1)$$

$$x^2 + 2y^2 = 18 \qquad (2)$$

Subtracting equation (1) from (2) we obtain

$$y^2 = 9, y = \pm 3.$$

By substituting the value of y into equation (1) or (2), we obtain

$$x_1 = 0 \text{ and } x_2 = 0.$$

So the solutions are

$$x = 0, y = 3 \text{ and } x = 0, y = -3.$$

C) **Two quadratic equations, one homogeneous**

An equation is said to be homogeneous if it is of the form

$$ax^2 + bxy + cy^2 + dx + ey = 0.$$

Consider the system

$$x^2 + 3xy + 2y^2 = 0 \qquad (1)$$

$$x^2 - 3xy + 2y^2 = 12 \qquad (2)$$

Equation (1) can be factored into the product of two linear equations.

$$x^2 + 3xy + 2y^2 = (x + 2y)(x + y) = 0$$

From this we determine that:

$$x + 2y = 0 \Rightarrow x = -2y$$

$$x + y = 0 \Rightarrow x = -y$$

Substituting $x = -2y$ into equation (2), we find:

$$(-2y)^2 - 3(-2y)y + 2y^2 = 12$$

$$4y^2 + 6y^2 + 2y^2 = 12$$

$$12y^2 = 12$$

$$y^2 = 1$$

$$y = \pm 1, \text{ so } x = \pm 2$$

Substituting $x = -y$ into equation (2) yields:

$$(-y)^2 - 3(-y)y + 2y^2 = 12$$

$$y^2 + 3y^2 + 2y^2 = 12$$

$$6y^2 = 12$$

$$y^2 = 2$$

$$y = \pm\sqrt{2}, \text{ so } x = \pm\sqrt{2}$$

So the solutions of equations (1) and (2) are

$$x = 2, y = -1, x = -2, y = 1, x = \sqrt{2},$$

$$y = -\sqrt{2}, \text{ and } x = -\sqrt{2}, y = \sqrt{2}.$$

D) **Two quadratic equations of the form**

$$ax^2 + bxy + cy^2 = d$$

Combine the two equations to obtain a homogeneous quadratic equation, then solve the equations by the third method.

E) **Two quadratic equations, each symmetrical in x and y**

Note: An equation is said to be symmetrical in x and y if by exchanging the coefficients of x and y we obtain the same equation. For example:

$$x^2 + y^2 = 9.$$

To solve systems involving this type of equation, substitute x by $u + v$ and y by $u - v$ and solve the resulting equations for u and v.

EXAMPLE

Given the system below:

$$x^2 + y^2 = 25 \tag{1}$$

$$x^2 + xy + y^2 = 37 \tag{2}$$

Substitute:

$$x = u + v$$

$$y = u - v$$

If we substitute the new values for x and y into equation (2), we obtain:

$$(u + v)^2 + (u + v)(u - v) + (u - v)^2 = 37$$

$$u^2 + 2uv + v^2 + u^2 - v^2 + u^2 - 2uv + v^2 = 37$$

$$3u^2 + v^2 = 37$$

If we substitute x and y into equation (1), we obtain:

$$(u + v)^2 + (u - v)^2 = 25$$

$$u^2 + 2uv + v^2 + u^2 - 2uv + v^2 = 25$$

$$2u^2 + 2v^2 = 25$$

The "new" system is:

$$3u^2 + v^2 = 34$$

$$2u^2 + 2v^2 = 25$$

which can be rewritten as:

$$3a + b = 37$$

$$2a + 2b = 25$$

and $\quad a = \dfrac{49}{4}, b = \dfrac{1}{4}.$

So $\quad u^2 = \dfrac{49}{4}$ and $v^2 = \dfrac{1}{4}$

$$u = \pm \frac{7}{2}$$

$$v = \pm \frac{1}{2}$$

$$x = \frac{7}{2} + \frac{1}{2} = 4 \text{ or } \frac{-7}{2} - \frac{1}{2} = -4$$

$$y = \frac{7}{2} - \frac{1}{2} = 3 \text{ or } \frac{-7}{2} + \frac{1}{2} = -3$$

The possible solutions are (4, 3), (–4, –3), (3, 4), (–3, –4).

Note that if the equation is symmetrical it is possible to interchange the solutions too. If $x = 3$, then $y = 4$ or vice-versa.

Quadratic Inequalities

To solve inequalities of the form

$$ax^2 + bx + c > 0$$

$$ax^2 + bx + c < 0$$

$$ax^2 + bx + c \geq 0$$

$$ax^2 + bx + c \leq 0$$

where $a > 0$, use the quadratic formula to obtain two roots r_1 and r_2 of $ax^2 + bx + c = 0$.

If r_1 and r_2 are complex, then $ax^2 + bx + c > 0$ for all x.

If r_1 and r_2 are real numbers such that $r_1 \neq r_2$ and $r_1 < r_2$, then

$$ax^2 + bx + c > 0 \qquad \text{if } x < r_1$$
$$ax^2 + bx + c = 0 \qquad \text{if } x = r_1$$
$$ax^2 + bx + c < 0 \qquad \text{if } r_1 < x < r_2$$
$$ax^2 + bx + c = 0 \qquad \text{if } x = r_2$$
$$ax^2 + bx + c > 0 \qquad \text{if } x > r_2$$

If r_1 and r_2 are real numbers such that $r_1 = r_2 = r$, then

$$ax^2 + bx + c > 0 \qquad \text{if } x < r$$
$$ax^2 + bx + c = 0 \qquad \text{if } x = r$$
$$ax^2 + bx + c > 0 \qquad \text{if } x > r$$

PROBLEM

Solve $-5x^2 + 9x + 2 < 0$.

SOLUTION

$-5x^2 + 9x + 2$ is not of the proper form since $-5 = a < 0$. So multiply by -1:

$$5x^2 - 9x - 2 > 0.$$

(Remember to switch the sense of the inequality.) Now the quadratic formula gives, with $a = 5$, $b = -9$, and c -2,

$$\frac{9 \pm \sqrt{81 - 4(5)(-2)}}{2(5)} = \frac{9 \pm 11}{10} = 2, \ -\frac{1}{5}$$

So $r_1 = -\frac{1}{5}$ and $r_2 = 2$. Therefore, $5x^2 - 9x - 2 > 0$ if $x < -\frac{1}{5}$ or $x > 2$.

EQUATIONS OF HIGHER ORDER

Methods to Solve Equations of Higher Order

A) **Factorization**

Given $x^4 - x = 0$.

By factorization it is possible to express this equation as

$$x(x^3 - 1) = 0.$$

The equation above can still be factored to give:

$$x(x - 1)(x^2 + x + 1) = 0,$$

which means that x, $(x - 1)$, or $(x^2 + x + 1)$ must be equal to zero.

$x = 0$ means 0 is a root of $x^4 - x = 0$.

$x - 1 = 0$ means 1 is a root.

To solve $x^2 + x + 1 = 0$, we can use the quadratic formula.

$$\frac{-1 \pm \sqrt{1^2 - 4(1)(1)}}{2(1)} = \frac{-1 \pm \sqrt{-3}}{2} = \frac{-1 \pm \sqrt{3}i}{2}$$

This implies

$$\frac{-1+\sqrt{3}i}{2} \text{ and } \frac{-1-\sqrt{3}i}{2}$$

are roots. So

$$\frac{-1+\sqrt{3}i}{2} \text{ and } \frac{-1-\sqrt{3}i}{2}$$

are solutions of $x^2 + x + 1 = 0$ and therefore of $x^4 - x = 0$. This means the solution set of $x^4 - x = 0$ is

$$\left\{ 0, 1, \frac{-1+\sqrt{3}i}{2}, \frac{-1-\sqrt{3}i}{2} \right\}.$$

B) If the equation to be solved is of third degree, it is possible to write it as:

$$x^3 + b_1 x^2 + b_2 x + b_3 = 0$$

where $-b_1$ = sum of the roots

b_2 = sum of the products of the roots taken two at a time

$(-1)^3 b_3$ = product of the roots

C) It is possible to determine the roots of an equation by writing the equation in the form: $y = f(x)$ and checking the values of x for which y is zero. These values of x are called zeros of the function and correspond to the roots. The figure below shows this procedure.

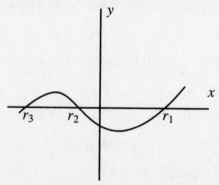

r_1, r_2, and r_3 can be determined by graphing the function $f(x)$ at a large number of points and connecting them. Note that the values read are just approximations of the roots.

D) If the equation to be solved is of fourth degree, we can substitute x^2 by y and solve a second degree equation using the quadratic formula. The square root of y would give the value of x. Note: This is only possible if the coefficient of x^3 is zero.

For example, solve $x^4 - 12x^2 + 8 = 0$.

$$x^4 - 12x^2 + 8 = (x^2)^2 - 12x^2 + 8 = 0$$

Let $x^2 = y$:

$$y^2 - 12y + 8 = 0$$

$$y = \frac{12 \pm \sqrt{144 - 4(1)(8)}}{2(1)}$$

$$y = 6 \pm 2\sqrt{7}$$

$$x = \pm\sqrt{6 \pm 2\sqrt{7}}$$

So the four roots are

$$+\sqrt{6 + 2\sqrt{7}} \; , \; -\sqrt{6 + 2\sqrt{7}} \; , \; +\sqrt{6 - 2\sqrt{7}} \; , \; -\sqrt{6 - 2\sqrt{7}} \; .$$

E) **Inspection**: Given an equation of any order greater than two; if it is possible to determine one of the roots r_1 by inspection, then $(x - r_1)$ is a factor. By dividing the polynomial by $(x - r_1)$, we can find other roots by factoring the quotient.

EXAMPLE

Find the roots of $x^4 + 2x^3 - 5x^2 - 4x + 6 = 0$. By inspection, $x = 1$ is a root.

So $(x - 1)$ is a factor and by dividing the polynomial by $(x - 1)$, we obtain:

$$
\begin{array}{r}
x^3 + 3x^2 - 2x - 6 \\
x - 1 \,) \overline{x^4 + 2x^3 - 5x^2 - 4x + 6} \\
\underline{-(x^4 - x^3)} \\
3x^3 - 5x^2 \\
\underline{-(3x^3 - 3x^2)} \\
-2x^2 - 4x \\
\underline{-(-2x^2 + 2x)} \\
(-6x + 6) \\
\underline{-(-6x + 6)} \\
0
\end{array}
$$

So we get $(x - 1)(x + 3)(x^2 - 2) = 0$. The roots of $x^4 + 2x^3 - 5x^2 - 4x + 6 = 0$ are $x = 1$, $x = -3$, and $x = \pm\sqrt{2}$.

Theory of Equations

A) **Remainder Theorem** – If a is any constant and if the polynomial $P(x)$ is divided by $(x - a)$, the remainder is $P(a)$.

EXAMPLE

Given a polynomial

$$2x^3 - x^2 + x + 4$$

divided by $x - 1$, the remainder is

$$2(1)^3 - (1)^2 + 1 + 4 = 6.$$

That is

$$2x^3 - x^2 + x + 4 = q(x) + \frac{6}{(x-1)}$$

where $q(x)$ is a polynomial.

Note that in this case $a = 1$.

B) **Factor Theorem** – If a is a root of the equation $f(x) = 0$, then $(x - a)$ is a factor of $f(x)$.

C) **Synthetic Division** – This method allows us to check if a certain constant c is a root of the given polynomial and, if it is not, it gives us the remainder of the division by $(x - c)$.

The general polynomial

$$P(x) = a_n x^n + a_{n-1} x^{n-1} + \ldots + a_i x^i + \ldots + a_0 x^0$$

can be represented by its coefficients a_i, written in descending powers of x.

The method consists of the following steps:

1) Write the coefficients a_i of the polynomial.

2) Multiply the first coefficient by the divisor and add it to the following coefficient of $P(x)$.

3) Continue until the last coefficient of $P(x)$ is reached. The resulting numbers are the coefficients of the quotient polynomial, with the last number representing the remainder. If the remainder is 0, then c is a root of $P(x)$.

Given $x^4 + 6x^3 - 2x^2 + 5$, divide by $x - (-1)$.

$$\frac{x^4 + 6x^3 - 2x^2 + 5}{x - 1}$$

$$
\begin{array}{r|rrrrr}
\boxed{1} & 6 & -2 & 0 & 5 & \underline{|-1} \\
 & -1 & & & & \\
\hline
1 & \boxed{5} & -2 & 0 & 5 & \underline{|-1} \\
 & & -5 & & & \\
\hline
1 & 5 & \boxed{-7} & 0 & 5 & \underline{|-1} \\
\end{array}
$$

Note that this can be written as:

$$x^4 + 6x^3 - 2x^2 + 0x + 5,$$

which explains the zero in the synthetic division.

$$
\begin{array}{r|rrrrr}
1 & 5 & -7 & 0 & 5 & \underline{|-1} \\
 & & & +7 & & \\
\hline
1 & 5 & -7 & \boxed{7} & 5 & \underline{|-1} \\
 & & & & -7 & \\
\hline
1 & 5 & -7 & 7 & \boxed{-2} & \\
\end{array}
$$

So the remainder is –2 and

$$\frac{x^4 + 6x^3 - 2x^2 + 5}{x - 1} = x^3 + 5x^2 - 7x + 7 - \frac{2}{x + 1}$$

Given $x^3 - 7x - 6$, check if 3 is a root:

$$
\begin{array}{r|rrrr}
\boxed{1} & 0 & -7 & -6 & \underline{|3} \\
 & 3 & & & \\
\hline
1 & \boxed{3} & -7 & -6 & \underline{|3} \\
 & & 9 & & \\
\hline
1 & 3 & \boxed{2} & -6 & \underline{|3} \\
 & & & +6 & \\
\hline
 & & & 0 & \\
\end{array}
$$

Yes, since the remainder is 0. Note that here x^2 has coefficient zero, which explains the zero in the synthetic division.

ALGEBRAIC THEOREMS

A) Every polynomial equation $f(x) = 0$ of degree greater than zero has at least one root either real or complex. This is known as the fundamental theorem of algebra.

B) Every polynomial equation of degree n has exactly n roots.

C) If a polynomial equation $f(x) = 0$ with real coefficients has a root $a + bi$, then the conjugate of this complex number $a - bi$ is also a root of $f(x) = 0$.

D) If $a + \sqrt{b}$ is a root of the polynomial equation $f(x) = 0$ with rational coefficients, then $a - \sqrt{b}$ is also a root, where a and b are rational and $\sqrt{b}$ is irrational.

E) If a rational fraction in lowest terms $\dfrac{b}{c}$ is a root of the equation

$$a_n x^n + a_{n-1} x^{n-1} + \ldots + a_1 x + a_0 = 0,$$

$a_0 \neq 0$, and the a_i are integers, then b is a factor of a, and c is a factor of a_n.

Furthermore, any rational roots of the equation below must be integers and factors of q_n.

$$x^n + q_1 x^{n-1} + q_2 x^{n-2} + \ldots + q_{n-1} x + q_n = 0$$

Note that $q_1, q_2, \ldots, q_n$ are integers.

Given

$$f(x) = a_n x^n + a_{n-1} x^{n-1} + \ldots + a_0 = 0$$

where $a_n, a_{n-1}, \ldots a_0$ are real and $a_n > 0$, q is an upper limit for all real roots of $f(x) = 0$ (a number q is called an upper limit for the real roots of $f(x) = 0$ if none of the roots is greater than q) if upon synthetic division of $f(x)$ by $x - q$, all of the numbers obtained in the last row* have the same sign. If, however, upon synthetic division of $f(x)$ by $x - p$, all of the numbers obtained in the last row* have alternating signs, then p is a lower limit for all the real roots of $f(x) = 0$. A number p is called a lower limit for the real roots if none of the roots is less than p.

*Note that the last row refers to the final line obtained by a synthetic division and corresponds to the line that gives the remainder.

F) Given a general polynomial of the form below:

$$f(x) = x^n + p_1 x^{n-1} + p_2 x^{n-2} + \ldots + p_{n-1} x + p_n = 0$$

It has the following properties:

a) $-p_1$ = sum of the roots

b) p_2 = sum of the products of the roots taken two at a time.

c) $-p_3$ = sum of the products of the roots taken three at a time.

d) $(-1)^n p_n$ = product of all the roots of $f(x) = 0$.

Descartes' Rule of Signs

Variation in sign: A polynomial $f(x)$ with real coefficients is said to have a variation in sign if after arranging its terms in descending powers of x, two successive terms differ in sign.

EXAMPLE

$$3x^5 - 4x^4 + 3x^3 - 9x^2 - x + 1$$

has four variations.

Descartes' Rule of Signs

The number of positive roots of a polynomial equation $f(x) = 0$ with real coefficients cannot exceed the number of variations in sign of $f(x)$. The difference between the number of variations and the number of positive roots of the equation is an even number.

The number of negative roots of $f(x) = 0$ cannot exceed the number of variations in sign of $f(-x)$. The difference between the number of variations and the number of negative roots is an even number.

EXAMPLE

$$3x^5 - 4x^4 + 3x^3 - x + 1 = 0$$

has four variations in sign so the number of positive roots cannot exceed 4. It can be 0, 2, or 4. $f(-x)$ would be obtained as shown below:

$$3(-x)^5 - 4(x)^4 + 3(-x)^3 - (-x) + 1 = 0$$

$$-3x^5 - 4x^4 - 3x^3 + x + 1$$

The number of variations equals 1, so the number of negative roots cannot exceed 1.

RATIO, PROPORTION, AND VARIATION

Ratio and Proportion

The ratio of two numbers x and y written $x:y$ is the fraction x/y where $y \neq 0$. A proportion is an equality of two ratios. The laws of proportion are listed below:

If $\dfrac{a}{b} = \dfrac{c}{d}$, then:

A) $ad = bc$

B) $\dfrac{b}{a} = \dfrac{d}{c}$

C) $\dfrac{a}{c} = \dfrac{b}{d}$

D) $\dfrac{a+b}{b} = \dfrac{c+d}{d}$

E) $\dfrac{a-b}{b} = \dfrac{c-d}{d}$

Given a proportion $a:b = c:d$, a and d are called the extremes, b and c are called the means, and d is called the fourth proportion to a, b, and c.

PROBLEM

Solve the proportion $\dfrac{x+1}{4} = \dfrac{15}{12}$.

SOLUTION

Cross multiply to determine x; that is, multiply the numerator of the first fraction by the denominator of the second, and equate this to the product of the numerator of the second and the denominator of the first.

$$(x+1)12 = 4 \times 15$$

$$12x + 12 = 60$$

$$x = 4$$

Variation

A) If x is directly proportional to y written $x \propto y$, then $x = ky$ or $\dfrac{x}{y} = k$, where k is called the constant of proportionality or the constant of variation.

B) If x varies inversely as y, then $x = \dfrac{k}{y}$.

C) If x varies jointly as y and z, then $x = kyz$.

PROBLEM

If y varies jointly as x and z, and $3x{:}1 = y{:}z$, find the constant of variation.

SOLUTION

A variable s is said to vary jointly as t and v if s varies directly as the product tv; that is, if $s = ctv$ where c is called the constant of variation.

Here the variable y varies jointly as x and z with k as the constant of variation.

$$y = kxz$$

$$3x{:}1 = y{:}z$$

Expressing these ratios as fractions.

$$\frac{3x}{1} = \frac{y}{z}$$

Solving for y by cross-multiplying,

$$y = 3xz$$

Equating both relations for y, we have:

$$kxz = 3xz$$

Solving for the constant of variation, k, we divide both sides by xz,

$$k = 3.$$

PRACTICE
TEST 1

CLEP COLLEGE ALGEBRA
Practice Test 1

(Answer sheets appear in the back of this book.)

TIME: 90 Minutes
70 Questions

DIRECTIONS: Solve each problem, using any available space on the page for scratch work. Then either enter the correct numerical answer in the box provided, or decide which answer choice is the best and fill in the corresponding oval on the answer sheet.

NOTES:

(1) Unless otherwise specified, the domain of any function f is assumed to be the set of all real numbers x for which $f(x)$ is a real number.

(2) i will be used to denote $\sqrt{-1}$.

(3) All figures lie in a plane and are drawn to scale unless otherwise indicated.

---

1. The solution set of $\dfrac{7}{x^2 + 8x + 23} = 1$ is

    (A) $\{8, 4\}$.   (D) $\{4, -4\}$.

    (B) $\{8, -4\}$.   (E) $\{16, 1\}$.

    (C) $\{-4, -4\}$.

2. Given the equation $\dfrac{7x}{3} = (a^4 + 1)^3$ and $a = -1$, solve for x.

    (A) 16   (D) $\dfrac{20}{3}$

    (B) $\dfrac{24}{7}$ (E) 0

    (C) 24

3. If $f(x) = 7x^2 + 3$ and $g(x) = 2x - 9$, then $g(f(2)) =$

(A) 28.

(D) 19.

(B) 0.

(E) 53.

(C) 31.

4. The solution set to the system

$$\begin{cases} 2x + 3y = 6 \\ y - 2 = -\dfrac{2x}{3} \end{cases}$$

is

(A) $\{0, 2\}$.

(B) $\{0, 0\}$.

(C) $\{\dfrac{1}{3}, 5\}$.

(D) $\{8, 3\}$.

(E) Infinite number of solutions.

5. When two resistances are installed in an electric circuit in parallel, the reciprocal of the resistance of the system is equal to the sum of the reciprocals of the parallel resistances. If r_1 and r_2 represent the resistances installed and R the resistance of the system, then

$$\frac{1}{R} = \frac{1}{r_1} + \frac{1}{r_2}.$$

What single resistance is the equivalent of resistances of 10 ohms and 25 ohms wired in parallel?

(A) .004 ohms

(D) 35 ohms

(B) 7.14 ohms

(E) 17.52 ohms

(C) 2.5 ohms

6. The number 120 is separated into two parts. The larger part exceeds three times the smaller by 12. The smaller part is

(A) 27.

(D) 39.

(B) 33.

(E) 29.

(C) 15

7. If $y = 3x$ lies in Quadrants I and III, then $y = |3x|$ lies in Quadrants

   (A) III and IV.

   (B) I and II.

   (C) I and III.

   (D) I, II, and III.

   (E) I only.

8. If a function is defined as $|2 - 5x| < 3$, then the interval which does not contain any solution for x is

   (A) $0 < x < 1$.

   (B) $0 < x < 2$.

   (C) $-\dfrac{1}{25} < x < 0$.

   (D) $-\dfrac{3}{5} < x < -\dfrac{1}{2}$.

   (E) $-1 < x < 1$.

9. For the following sequence of numbers, $\dfrac{1}{2}, \dfrac{1}{12}, \dfrac{1}{30}, \ldots$, the next number will be

   (A) $\dfrac{1}{36}$.

   (B) $\dfrac{1}{27}$.

   (C) $\dfrac{1}{48}$.

   (D) $\dfrac{1}{56}$.

   (E) $\dfrac{1}{72}$.

10. A supermarket, rectangular in shape and 200 feet by 300 feet, is to be built on a city block that contains 81,600 square feet. There will be a uniform strip around the building for parking. How wide is the strip?

    (A) 27 ft.

    (B) 15 ft.

    (C) 33.3 ft.

    (D) 20 ft.

    (E) 12 ft.

11. If $m \neq 0$, then $(25)^{3m}(125)^{8m}(5)^m$ can be expressed as

    (A) 125^{12m}.

    (B) 5^{20m}.

    (C) 5^{19m}.

    (D) 25^{12m}.

    (E) 5^{31m}.

12. The roots of $x^2 + 2x + 5 = 0$ are

(A) 3, 4.

(D) 6, 3.

(B) $-1 \pm 2i$.

(E) $2 \pm 3i$.

(C) $3 \pm 4i$.

13. What is the range of values for which $|6x - 5| \leq 8$ is satisfied?

(A) $-\dfrac{1}{2} \leq x \leq \dfrac{1}{2}$

(D) $-\dfrac{1}{2} \leq x \leq \dfrac{13}{6}$

(B) $0 \leq x \leq \dfrac{5}{6}$

(E) $-\dfrac{1}{2} \leq x \leq \dfrac{1}{3}$

(C) $-1 \leq x \leq \dfrac{1}{2}$

14. Two cars are traveling 40 and 50 miles per hour, respectively. If the second car starts out five miles behind the first car, how many minutes will it take the second car to overtake the first car?

15. If $f(x) = 7x - 8$ and $-5 \leq x \leq 8$, what is the range of $f(x)$?

(A) $-25 \leq y \leq 15$

(D) $-15 \leq y \leq 20$

(B) $-43 \leq y \leq 0$

(E) $-43 \leq y \leq 48$

(C) $-30 \leq y \leq 12$

16. If $i = \sqrt{-1}$, then $(a + bi)^2 - (a - bi)^2$ is equivalent to

(A) $4abi$.

(D) $2bi$.

(B) -1.

(E) $-2b^2$.

(C) $a^2 - b^2$.

17. The fraction

$$\frac{\dfrac{2}{b^2 a^2}}{\dfrac{1}{b^2 - 2b}}$$

may be expressed more simply as

(A) $\dfrac{2a}{b}$.

(D) $\dfrac{b-a}{a}$.

(B) $\dfrac{b-4}{b}$.

(E) $\dfrac{2b-4}{ba^2}$.

(C) $\dfrac{ab}{b^2 - a}$.

18. Reserved seat tickets to a football game are $6 more than general admission tickets. Mr. Jones finds that he can buy general admission tickets for his whole family of five for only $3 more than the cost of reserved seat tickets for himself and Mrs. Jones. How much do the general admission tickets cost?

(A) $11.00

(D) $5.00

(B) $9.00

(E) $4.00

(C) $12.00

19. If $\log_8 N = \dfrac{2}{3}$, what is the value of N?

20. The equation $x^2 + 2x + 7 = 0$ has

(A) two complex conjugate roots.

(B) two real rational roots.

(C) two real equal roots.

(D) two rational equal roots.

(E) two real irrational roots.

21. The equation $x = 3y + 8$ has a y-intercept of

    (A) $\dfrac{1}{2}$.

    (B) 8.

    (C) $-\dfrac{8}{3}$.

    (D) -8.

    (E) 16.

22. A function is defined as $f(x) = x^2 + 2$. What is the numerical value of $3f(0) + f(-1)f(2)$?

    (A) 6

    (B) 24

    (C) 18

    (D) 4

    (E) 36

23. What value must x take on in order for the following equation to be true?
    $$\frac{7}{x+3} = \frac{8}{x+5}$$

    (A) 3

    (B) 5

    (C) 7

    (D) 8

    (E) 11

24. The pressure of wind on a sail varies directly as the area of the sail and the square of the wind's velocity. When the wind is 15 miles per hour, the force on a square foot is one pound. What is the velocity of the wind when the force on a square yard is 25 pounds?

    (A) 5

    (B) 45

    (C) 8

    (D) 40

    (E) 15

25. If $x = (y + 4)^2$ and $y = -7$, what is x?

    ┌─────────────┐
    │   │
    └─────────────┘

26. If $2^{3x} = 64$, then $x =$

   (A) 1.   (D) $\dfrac{5}{2}$.

   (B) $\dfrac{3}{2}$.   (E) 3.

   (C) 2.

27. If $5 < a < 8$ and $6 < b < 9$, then

   (A) $45 < ab < 48$.   (D) $54 < ab < 72$.

   (B) $30 < ab < 45$.   (E) $5 < ab < 72$.

   (C) $30 < ab < 72$.

28. If $\dfrac{a}{b} = 4$, then what is $a^2 - 16b^2$?

   (A) -16 (D) 4

   (B) -4 (E) 16

   (C) 0

29. If $xy - 3x = 20$ and $y - 3 = 5$, then $x =$

   (A) 20.   (D) 4.

   (B) 15.   (E) 3.

   (C) 5.

30. $\sqrt{8} + 3\sqrt{18} - 7\sqrt{2} =$

   (A) $3 - 3\sqrt{2}$ (D) $4\sqrt{2}$

   (B) 0   (E) $10\sqrt{2}$

   (C) $6\sqrt{2} - 4\sqrt{3}$

31. A purse contains 19 coins worth $3.40. If the purse contains only dimes and quarters, how many of each coin are in the purse?

   (A) 8 dimes, 12 quarters

   (B) 10 dimes, 9 quarters

(C) 9 dimes, 10 quarters

(D) 5 dimes, 6 quarters

(E) 12 dimes, 8 quarters

32. If an operation * is defined for all real numbers a and b by the equation $a * b = a - b + ab$. Find $3*(-3)$.

(A) -9 (D) 3

(B) -3 (E) 9

(C) 0

33. If $f(x) = 4x - 1$ and $1 < x < 4$, then $f(x)$ is between

(A) 0 and 1.   (D) 3 and 15.

(B) 0 and 3.   (E) 0 and 15.

(C) 1 and 15.

34. What is the solution set of $|3x - 9| < 5$?

(A) $\dfrac{4}{3} < x < \dfrac{8}{3}$ (D) $\dfrac{4}{3} < x < \dfrac{13}{3}$

(B) $-\dfrac{4}{3} < x < \dfrac{7}{3}$ (E) $\dfrac{4}{3} < x < \dfrac{14}{3}$

(C) $-\dfrac{4}{3} < x < \dfrac{8}{3}$

35. A man can do a job in nine days and his son can do the same job in 16 days. They start working together. After four days the son leaves and the father finishes the job alone. How many days did the man take to finish the job alone?

(A) $2\dfrac{3}{4}$ (D) $2\dfrac{1}{4}$

(B) $1\dfrac{1}{2}$ (E) $3\dfrac{1}{2}$

(C) $3\dfrac{3}{4}$

36. If $x \neq 0$, then $(3^{9x})(27^{2x}) =$

    (A) 2^{5x}.   (D) 3^{18x}.

    (B) 9^{3x}.   (E) 3^{9x}.

    (C) 3^{15x}.

37. If $f(x) = 3x + 2$ and $g(f(x)) = x$, then $g(x) =$

    (A) $\dfrac{x-2}{3}$.   (D) $3x - 2$.

    (B) $\dfrac{x}{3} - 2$.   (E) $4x + 9$.

    (C) $3x$.

38. Find the smallest positive integer which is divisible by both 12 and 15.

    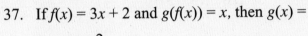

39. Let $n(A)$ denote the number of elements in set A. If $n(A) = 10$, $n(B) = 12$, and $n(A \cap B) = 3$, how many elements does $A \cup B$ contain?

40. Find the solution set of the following equation:

    $|3x - 2| = 7$

    (A) $\{-\dfrac{5}{3}\}$ (D) $\{-\dfrac{7}{3}, 3\}$

    (B) $\{-\dfrac{5}{3}, -\dfrac{7}{3}\}$ (E) $\{3, -\dfrac{5}{3}\}$

    (C) $\{3\}$

41. A mechanic and his helper repair a car in eight hours. The mechanic works three times as fast as his helper. How long would it take the helper to make the repair, working alone?

    (A) 27 hrs.   (D) 32 hrs.

    (B) 1 hr. and 15 min.   (E) 6 hrs.

    (C) 13 hrs. and 10 min.

42. Find the solution set of the following pair of equations:
$$\begin{cases} 3x + 4y = -6 \\ 5x + 6y = -8 \end{cases}$$

    (A) $\{(1, 2)\}$ (D) $\{(2, -3)\}$

    (B) $\{(1, 3)\}$ (E) $\{(3, -3)\}$

    (C) $\{(2, 3)\}$

43. If $\dfrac{7}{x+4} = \dfrac{5}{x+6}$, then $x =$

    (A) -11.   (D) 7.

    (B) -7.   (E) 11.

    (C) 5.

44. If $\log_2 (x - 1) + \log_2 (x + 1) = 3$, then $x =$

    (A) -1.   (D) 3.

    (B) 1.   (E) 4.

    (C) 2.

45. $10^x = 31.4$, then $x =$

    (A) 0.   (D) 3.14.

    (B) 1.   (E) 31.4.

    (C) 1.50.

46. If $f(x) = 3x^2 - x + 5$, what is the value of $f(3)$?

                             [   ]

47. If $-9 < x < -4$ and $-12 < y < -6$, then

    (A) $0 < xy < 12$.   (D) $10 < xy < 24$.

    (B) $108 < xy < 112$.   (E) $4 < xy < 12$.

    (C) $24 < xy < 108$.

48. Two cars travel at 40 and 60 miles per hour, respectively. If the second car starts out five miles behind the first car, how long will it take the second car to overtake the first car?

(A) $\dfrac{1}{2}$ hr.   (D) $\dfrac{1}{5}$ hr.

(B) $\dfrac{1}{4}$ hr.   (E) Cannot be determined.

(C) 1 hr.

49. $\sqrt{108} + 3\sqrt{12} - 7\sqrt{3} =$

(A) $3 - 3\sqrt{3}$ (D) $5\sqrt{3}$

(B) 0   (E) $10\sqrt{3}$

(C) $4\sqrt{3}$

50. What is the solution to the pair of equations below?

$$\begin{cases} x - 3y = 1 \\ 2x + y = 2 \end{cases}$$

(A) $x = 1$ and $y = 0$ (D) $x = 0$ and $y = 1$

(B) $x = 2$ and $y = 0$ (E) $x = 0$ and $y = 2$

(C) $x = 3$ and $y = 1$

51. If x and y are positive integers, which of the following must be a positive integer?

I. $x + y$

II. $x - y$

III. xy

(A) I only   (D) I and III only

(B) II only   (E) I, II, and III

(C) I and II only

52. If $\log_8 x = \dfrac{4}{3}$, what is the value of x?

☐

53. The solution set for x in the inequality $|x^2 - 3| < 1$ is

   (A) $\{x \mid -\sqrt{2} < x < \sqrt{2}\}$.

   (B) $\{x \mid -2 < x < -\sqrt{2}\}$.

   (C) $\{x \mid -2 < x < -\sqrt{2} \text{ or } \sqrt{2} < x < 2\}$.

   (D) $\{x \mid -\sqrt{2} < x < \sqrt{2} \text{ or } -2 < x < 2\}$.

   (E) $\{x \mid \sqrt{2} < x < 2\}$.

54. If $\log_8 3 = x\log_2 3$, then x equals

   (A) 4.   (D) $\log_4 3$.

   (B) 3.   (E) $\dfrac{1}{3}$.

   (C) $\log_8 9$.

55. There are six knights of the round table. Given that Sir Lancelot must sit in a specific chair and that Sir Gawain must be directly on either side of him, in how many ways may the knights be seated?

☐

56. $\log_3(81)^{-2.3} =$

   (A) 8.0   (D) −9.2

   (B) 3.0   (E) −4.5

   (C) 5.6

57. $\log_2 \dfrac{\sqrt{2}}{8} =$

    (A) $\dfrac{5}{2}$ (D) $-\dfrac{5}{2}$

    (B) $\dfrac{1}{2}$ (E) $-\dfrac{1}{2}$

    (C) $\dfrac{3}{2}$

58. A rectangular solid has dimensions 3, 4, and 5. Find its diagonal.

    (A) 4.33   (D) 5.25

    (B) 9.41   (E) 7.07

    (C) 3.14

59. What is the slope of the line

$$15x + 37y - 23 = 0?$$

    (A) 0.405   (D) 2.467

    (B) -0.405 (E) 15

    (C) 37

60. What is the equation of the line which is parallel to $6x + 3y = 4$ and has a y-intercept of -6?

    (A) $y = -2x + \dfrac{4}{3}$ (D) $y = -2x - 6$

    (B) $y = 2x + \dfrac{4}{3}$ (E) $y = -2x + 6$

    (C) $y = -2x - \dfrac{4}{3}$

TEST STOPS HERE. *EXTRA PRACTICE FOLLOWS...*

61. $\dfrac{\sqrt[3]{-16}}{\sqrt[3]{-2}} =$

(A) 2

(D) $\sqrt[3]{2}$

(B) –2

(E) $\sqrt[3]{-2}$

(C) $2\sqrt{3}$

62. An airplane with an air speed of 300 miles per hour flies against a head wind, and flies 900 miles in four hours. What is the speed of the head wind?

(A) 900 mph

(D) 300 mph

(B) 75 mph

(E) 150 mph

(C) 50 mph

63. If $f(x) = 2x + 4$ and $g(x) = x^2 - 2$, then $(f \circ g)(x)$, where $(f \circ g)(x)$ is a composition of functions, is

(A) $2x^2 - 8$.

(D) $2x^3 + 4x^2 - 4x - 8$.

(B) $2x^2 + 8$.

(E) $4x^2 + 16x + 14$.

(C) $2x^2$.

64. Given $\log_{10} 2 = 0.3010$, find $\log_{10} 32$.

(A) 0.6020

(D) 30.10

(B) 3.010

(E) 0.03010

(C) 1.5050

65. If $f(x) = x - 2x^2 + 2$, then $f(a - 2) =$

(A) $(a - 2)^2 + 2$.

(D) $3a^2 - 9a + 8$.

(B) $9a - 2a^2 - 8$.

(E) $-9a + 2a^2 - 8$.

(C) $2a^2 + 10a - 8$.

66. If $b^2 - 4c = 0$, where b and c are real numbers, then the roots of the

equation

$$x^2 + bx + c = 0$$

are

(A) real and equal.

(D) complex and unequal.

(B) real and unequal.

(E) No solution.

(C) complex and equal.

67. A cube has a total surface area of 24 cm². What is the volume of the cube in cm³?

68. If $f(x) = \sqrt{x+1}$ and $g(x) = x^3 + 2$, find $f(g(2))$.

(A) 3.32

(D) 10.9

(B) 2.9

(E) 4.2

(C) 7.1

69. $\lim\limits_{x \to 0} \left(\dfrac{x^2 - 2x}{x} \right) =$

(A) −2

(D) 2

(B) 0

(E) Does not exist.

(C) 1

70. If $f(x) = 3x - 5$ and $g(f(x)) = x$, then $g(x) =$

(A) $\dfrac{x-5}{3}$.

(D) $\dfrac{x+5}{4}$.

(B) $\dfrac{x+5}{3}$.

(E) $\dfrac{5-x}{3}$.

(C) $\dfrac{2x+5}{3}$.

CLEP COLLEGE ALGEBRA
TEST 1

ANSWER KEY

1.	(C)	19.	(4)	37.	(A)	55.	(48)
2.	(B)	20.	(A)	38.	(60)	56.	(D)
3.	(E)	21.	(C)	39.	(19)	57.	(D)
4.	(E)	22.	(B)	40.	(E)	58.	(E)
5.	(B)	23.	(E)	41.	(D)	59.	(B)
6.	(A)	24.	(C)	42.	(D)	60.	(D)
7.	(B)	25.	(9)	43.	(A)	61.	(A)
8.	(D)	26.	(C)	44.	(D)	62.	(B)
9.	(D)	27.	(C)	45.	(C)	63.	(C)
10.	(D)	28.	(C)	46.	(29)	64.	(C)
11.	(E)	29.	(D)	47.	(C)	65.	(B)
12.	(B)	30.	(D)	48.	(B)	66.	(A)
13.	(D)	31.	(C)	49.	(D)	67.	(8)
14.	(30)	32.	(B)	50.	(A)	68.	(A)
15.	(E)	33.	(D)	51.	(D)	69.	(A)
16.	(A)	34.	(E)	52.	(16)	70.	(B)
17.	(E)	35.	(A)	53.	(C)		
18.	(D)	36.	(C)	54.	(E)		

DETAILED EXPLANATIONS
OF ANSWERS
TEST 1

1. **(C)**

$$\frac{7}{x^2 + 8x + 23} = 1$$

Multiply both sides by $x^2 + 8x + 23$:

$$x^2 + 8x + 23 = 7$$

Subtract 7 from both sides:

$$x^2 + 8x + 16 = 0$$

Factor:

$$(x + 4)(x + 4) = 0$$

Solution set $\{-4, -4\}$

2. **(B)**

$$\frac{7}{3}x = (a^4 + 1)^3$$

Substituting $a = -1$ we obtain:

$$\frac{7}{3}x = (1 + 1)^3 = 8$$

Multiplying both sides by $3/7$ we solve the equation for x, i.e., $x = {}^{24}/_7$.

3. **(E)**

$$f(x) = 7x^2 + 3, \ g(x) = 2x - 9$$

Substituting 2 into $f(x)$:

$f(2) = 7(2)^2 + 3 = 31.$

So $g(f(2)) = g(31).$

Substituting and solving:

$g(31) = 2(31) - 9 = 53$

4. **(E)**

$2x + 3y = 6$

$y - 2 = -\dfrac{2x}{3}$

Multiplying the second equation by 3, we obtain:

$3y - 6 = 2x$

Transposing, we obtain:

$2x + 3y = 6$

Thus, both equations are equivalent and define one straight line. Since they intersect at every point, there are an infinite number of solutions.

5. **(B)**   Let $r_1 = 10$ ohms and $r_2 = 25$ ohms. We are looking for the single resistance R, which is equivalent to r_1 and r_2.

The reciprocal of R $= \dfrac{1}{R}$

The reciprocal of r_1 $= \dfrac{1}{r_1}$

The reciprocal of r_2 $= \dfrac{1}{r_2}$

Now substitute the values for r_1 and r_2, respectively, into the equation. Thus,

$\dfrac{1}{R} = \dfrac{1}{10} + \dfrac{1}{25}$

Add the fractions according to the rule:

$$\frac{a}{b} + \frac{c}{d} = \frac{ad + bc}{bd}$$

$$\frac{1}{R} = \frac{25 + 10}{250} = \frac{35}{250}$$

$$R = \frac{250}{35} = \frac{50}{7} = 7.14 \text{ ohms}$$

6.   **(A)**

Let x = larger number

y = smaller number

$x + y = 120$

$x = 3y + 12$

This system is solved for y.

Substituting:

$3y + 12 + y = 120$

$4y = 108$

Dividing by 4:

$y = 27$

7.   **(B)**

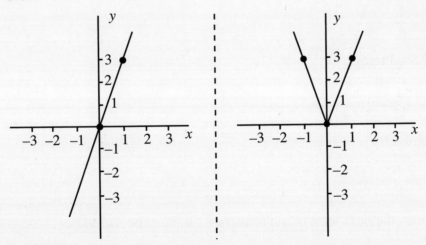

When taking the absolute value of a function, all negative function values are made positive. Positive *y* values are defined for Quadrants I and II. Negative values are in Quadrants III and IV. Therefore, the defined function must lie in Quadrants I and II only.

8.   **(D)**   The inequality $|\,2-5x\,| < 3$ may be rewritten as

$$-3 < 2 - 5x < 3.$$

Subtracting 2 from each side, we obtain:

$$-5 < -5x < 1$$

Dividing by -5 gives:

$$-\frac{1}{5} < x < 1$$

This is the interval over which all solutions lie. We are looking for an interval which does not contain any solutions to the inequality. The only interval given in the choices that satisfies this criterion is

$$-\frac{3}{5} < x < -\frac{1}{2}.$$

9.   **(D)**   To determine the next number, we look for a pattern among the previous terms. Only the denominators differ. We note by inspection that each denominator is equal to the product of two successive integers. For example,

the first term:

$$\frac{1}{2} = \frac{1}{1 \times 2}$$

the second term:

$$\frac{1}{12} = \frac{1}{3 \times 4}$$

the third term:

$$\frac{1}{30} = \frac{1}{5 \times 6}$$

Thus, the next term in the sequence can be expected to be

$$\frac{1}{7 \times 8} = \frac{1}{56}.$$

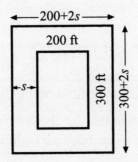

10. **(D)**   If the strip is s feet wide, the dimensions of the supermarket will be $200 + 2s$ by $300 + 2s$ (see figure). Its area, the product of the width and length, is $(200 + 2s)(300 + 2s)$ square feet. But the area is given as 81,600 square feet. Thus, we have

$$(200 + 2s)(300 + 2s) = 81,600$$

$$60,000 + 1,000s + 4s^2 = 81,600$$

$$4s^2 + 1,000s - 21,600 = 0 \qquad \text{Standard Quadratic Form}$$

Dividing by 4:

$$s^2 + 250s - 5,400 = 0$$

Using the quadratic formula,

$$s = \frac{-b \pm \sqrt{b^2 - 4ac}}{2a}$$

with $a = 1$, $b = 250$, and $c = -5,400$, we have:

$$s = \frac{-250 \pm \sqrt{250^2 + 21,600}}{2}$$

$$s = \frac{-250 \pm 290}{2}$$

$$s = 20 \text{ or } s = -270$$

The strip is 20 feet wide, since it is impossible for a strip to be a negative width.

Check: If the strip is 20 feet wide, then the block is 340 by 240 feet, and its area must be (340) (240) = 81,600 square feet.

11. **(E)**   We use the laws of exponents to solve this problem. $(25)^{3m}$ can be expressed as $(5^2)^{3m}$, which can also be written as 5^{6m}.

   $(125)^{8m}$ can, by a similar argument, be expressed as 5^{24m}.

When we multiply a number of the same base raised to different powers, we simply keep the same base and add the exponents. Thus:

$$(25)^{3m}(125)^{8m}(5)^m = 5^{6m}5^{24m}5^m = 5^{31m}$$

12. **(B)**   The polynomial is not factorable, so we must use the quadratic formula:

$$x = \frac{-b \pm \sqrt{b^2 - 4ac}}{2a}$$

In the polynomial, $a = 1$, $b = 2$, and $c = 5$. Substituting, we get:

$$x = \frac{-2 \pm \sqrt{2^2 - 4(1)(5)}}{2(1)}$$

Simplifying:

$$x = \frac{-2 \pm \sqrt{-16}}{2} = \frac{-2 \pm 4\sqrt{-1}}{2} = -1 \pm 2\sqrt{-1}$$

We know $\sqrt{-1} = i$, so:

$$x = -1 \pm 2i.$$

13. **(D)**   When given an inequality with an absolute value, recall the definition of absolute value:

$$|x| \equiv \begin{cases} x \text{ if } x \geq 0 \\ -x \text{ if } x < 0 \end{cases}$$

   $6x - 5 \leq 8$ if $6x - 5 \geq 0$

   $-6x + 5 \leq 8$ if $6x - 5 < 0$

   $-6x + 5 \leq 8$ can be written as $6x - 5 \geq -8$.

We can set up both of these equations as follows:

$$-8 \le 6x - 5 \le 8$$

Adding 5:

$$-3 \le 6x \le 13$$

Dividing by 6:

$$-\frac{1}{2} \le x \le \frac{13}{6}$$

So the values of x which satisfy $|6x - 5| \le 8$ are

$$\left[-\frac{1}{2}, \frac{13}{6}\right].$$

14. **(30)**

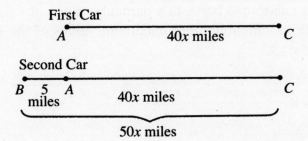

Let x = number of hours it takes the second car to overtake the first car.

	Rate (in mph)	Time (hours)	Distance (miles)
First Car	40	x	$40x$
Second Car	50	x	$50x$

Distance = rate × time

Then $50x$ = distance second car travels in x hours,

and $40x$ = distance first car travels in x hours.

Since the second car must travel an additional five miles (from B to A in diagram).

$$40x + 5 = 50x$$

Simplify,

$$-10x = -5$$

Divide by -10,

$$x = \frac{1}{2},$$

number of hours it takes the second car to overtake the first car.

Check:

$$40\left(\frac{1}{2}\right) + 5 = 50\left(\frac{1}{2}\right)$$

$$25 = 25$$

15. **(E)**   We are given the domain of $f(x)$ as $-5 \le x \le 8$. This domain corresponds, on a one-to-one basis, to a particular range of values. Given $f(x)$, we substitute the minimum and maximum values of the domain to find the required range.

Function:

$$f(x) = 7x - 8$$

Substituting -5 for x:

$$f(-5) = 7(-5) - 8 = -35 - 8 = -43$$

The lower limit is -43.

Substituting 8 for x:

$$f(8) = 7(8) - 8 = 56 - 8 = 48$$

The upper limit is 48.

Therefore, the range is:

$$-43 \le y \le 48$$

16. **(A)**   This problem illustrates the manipulation of complex numbers. First evaluate $(a + bi)^2$:

$$(a + bi)^2 = (a + bi)(a + bi) = a^2 + abi + abi + b^2 i^2$$

Since $i^2 = -1$, $(a + bi)^2 = a^2 - b^2 + 2abi$

Next, evaluate $(a - bi)^2$:

$$(a - bi)^2 = (a - bi)(a - bi) = a^2 - abi - abi + b^2i^2$$

This is equivalent to:

$$a^2 - b^2 - 2abi.$$

When subtracting complex numbers, we subtract the two real parts and the two imaginary parts separately. So,

$$(a + bi)^2 - (a - bi)^2 = [(a^2 - b^2) + 2abi] - [(a^2 - b^2) - 2abi]$$

$a^2 - b^2$ disappears and we are left with:

$$2abi - (-2abi) = 4abi$$

17. **(E)**   The fraction is a complex fraction. To simplify, we must multiply both the numerator and denominator by $b^2 - 2b$:

$$\frac{\dfrac{2}{a^2b^2}}{\dfrac{1}{b^2 - 2b}} \times \frac{b^2 - 2b}{b^2 - 2b} = \frac{2(b^2 - 2b)}{a^2b^2}$$

Multiplying through in the numerator:

$$\frac{2b^2 - 4b}{a^2b^2}$$

The numerator is factored and like terms are cancelled:

$$\frac{b(2b - 4)}{a^2b^2} = \frac{2b - 4}{a^2b}$$

18. **(D)**

Let x = the cost of general admission tickets.

Let $x + 6$ = the cost of reserved seat tickets.

Thus, $5x$ is the cost of five general admission tickets and $2(x + 6)$ is the cost of two reserved seat tickets. Since the five tickets cost $3.00 more than the two reserved tickets,

$$5x = 2(x + 6) + 3$$

$$5x = 2x + 12 + 3$$

$$5x = 2x + 15$$

$$3x = 15$$

$$x = 5$$

and $x + 6 = 5 + 6 = 11$

Thus, general admission tickets are \$5.00, and reserve tickets are \$11.00.

19. **(4)**   To solve, the inverse of the logarithmic function must be used. This is stated as:

$$y = \log_a N$$

$$N = a^y$$

Applying this to the given equation yields $N = 8^{2/3}$. So

$$N = \sqrt[3]{8^2} = \sqrt[3]{64} = 4.$$

20. **(A)**   To solve this quadratic equation, we invoke the quadratic formula:

$$x = \frac{-b \pm \sqrt{b^2 - 4ac}}{2a}$$

The equation is $x^2 + 2x + 7 = 0$.

So $a = 1$, $b = 2$, and $c = 7$.

Substituting into the formula:

$$x = \frac{-2 \pm \sqrt{2^2 - 4(1)(7)}}{2(1)}$$

$$= \frac{-2 \pm \sqrt{4 - 28}}{2} = -1 \pm \sqrt{-6}$$

Since $i = \sqrt{-1}$, $x = -1 \pm i\sqrt{6}$.

These roots are complex conjugates of each other.

21. **(C)**   The simplest way to solve is to get the equation into slope intercept form: $y = mx + b$, where m is the slope and b is the y-intercept. The given equation is:

$$x = 3y + 8$$

Subtracting 8 from both sides:

$$3y = x - 8$$

Dividing by 3:

$$y = \frac{1}{3}x - \frac{8}{3}$$

From this and the slope intercept form, $b = -8/3$. Thus, the y-intercept is $-8/3$.

22. **(B)** We are given $f(x) = x^2 + 2$. We must find $f(0)$, $f(-1)$, and $f(2)$.

Replacing x with zero, we obtain:

$$f(0) = 0^2 + 2 = 2$$

Similarly:

$$f(-1) = (-1)^2 + 2 = 3$$

Finally:

$$f(2) = (2)^2 + 2 = 6$$

Evaluating:

$$3f(0) + f(-1)f(2) = 3(2) + (3)(6)$$
$$= 6 + 18 = 24$$

23. **(E)**

$$\frac{7}{x+3} = \frac{8}{x+5}$$

Cross multiplying:

$$7x + 35 = 8x + 24$$

Subtracting $7x$ on both sides:

$$35 = x + 24$$

Subtracting 24 on both sides:

$$x = 11$$

24. **(C)**

Let p = pressure of the wind, in pounds per unit area

v = the velocity of the wind, in miles per hour

a = the area of the sail, in square feet

Pressure, p, varies directly as the area of the sail, a, and the square of the wind's velocity, v^2. Therefore, p varies directly as the product av^2 times a proportionality constant, k. k must be determined before we can proceed to find v as desired. Use the given information $a = 1$ and $p = 1$ when $v = 15$ mph $= 22$ ft. per second, to determine the proportionality constant, k.

$$p = kav^2$$

$$1 = k(1)(22)^2$$

$$k = \frac{1}{484}, \text{ value of the proportionality constant.}$$

Now we can find v using $k = \dfrac{1}{484}$ when $p = 25$ lbs. and $a = 9$ sq. ft. (1 yard = 3 feet, 1 square yard = 9 square feet).

$$p = \frac{1}{484}av^2.$$

$$\frac{25}{9\text{ft}^2} = \frac{1}{484}(9)v^2.$$

$$v^2 = \frac{(25)484}{9 \times 9}$$

$$v = \sqrt{\frac{(25)(484)}{9}} = 12.2\frac{\text{ft.}}{\text{sec.}} = 8\frac{\text{mi.}}{\text{hr.}}$$

$v = 8$, number of miles per hour

25. **(9)**

$$x = (y + 4)^2$$

Substitute $y = -7$ into the equation:

$$x = (-7 + 4)^2$$

$$x = (-3)^2$$

$$x = 9$$

26. **(C)**

$$2^{3x} = 64$$

$$(2^3)^x = 64$$

$$(8)^x = 64$$

$$x = 2$$

27. **(C)** If $5 < a < 8$ and $6 < b < 9$, then ab will be bounded by (5×6) and (8×9).

28. **(C)**

$$\frac{a}{b} = 4$$

Multiplying both sides by b:

$$a = 4b$$

$$a^2 - 16b^2 = (4b)^2 - 16b^2$$

Substituting $a = 4b$:

$$= 0$$

29. **(D)**

$$xy - 3x = 20$$

Factor:

$$x(y - 3) = 20$$

Substituting $(y - 3) = 5$:

$$x(5) = 20$$

Dividing both sides by 5:

$$x = 4$$

30. **(D)**

$$\sqrt{8} + 3\sqrt{18} - 7\sqrt{2} = \sqrt{4} \times \sqrt{2} + 3\sqrt{9} \times \sqrt{2} - 7\sqrt{2}$$
$$= 2\sqrt{2} + 9\sqrt{2} - 7\sqrt{2}$$
$$= 4\sqrt{2}$$

31. **(C)**

Let x = the number of dimes in the purse

Then $19 - x$ = the number of quarters in the purse

$10x$ = the value of the dimes

$25(19 - x)$ = the value of quarters

The relationship used in setting up the equation is:

The value of the dimes + the value of the quarters = $3.40

$$10x + 25(19 - x) = 340$$
$$10x + 475 - 25x = 340$$
$$x = 9$$

There are 9 dimes and 10 quarters in the purse.

Check: The dimes are worth $.90 and the quarters are worth $2.50, making a total of $3.40.

32. **(B)**   Substitute $a = 3$ and $b = -3$ into the given equation:

$$3 \times (-3) = 3 - (-3) + 3(-3)$$
$$= 3 + 3 - 9$$
$$= -3$$

33. **(D)**

For $x = 1$, $f(x) = 3$

For $x = 4$, $f(x) = 15$

34. **(E)**

$$|3x - 9| < 5$$

$$-5 < (3x - 9) < 5$$

$$-\frac{5}{3} < x - 3 < \frac{5}{3}$$

$$\frac{4}{3} < x < \frac{14}{3}$$

35. **(A)** Let x = the number of days it takes the man to finish the job.

Note that the man actually works $(x + 4)$ days, and the son actually works 4 days.

The relationship used to set up the equation is: Part of job done by man + Part of job done by boy = 1 job

$$\frac{x+4}{9} + \frac{4}{16} = 1$$

$$16(x + 4) + 4(9) = 144$$

$$x = 2\frac{3}{4} \text{ days}$$

Check:

$$\frac{2\frac{3}{4} + 4}{9} + \frac{4}{16} = 1$$

$$\frac{3}{4} + \frac{1}{4} = 1$$

36. **(C)**

$$(3^{9x})(27^{2x}) = (3^{9x})(3^3)^{2x}$$

$$= (3^{9x})(3^{6x})$$

$$= 3^{9x+6x}$$

$$= 3^{15x}$$

37. **(A)**

    Let $y = f(x) = 3x + 2$.

    Then, $\quad x = \dfrac{y-2}{3}$.

    Therefore, $\quad g(x) = \dfrac{x-2}{3}$.

38. **(60)**

    $$12 = 2 \times 2 \times 3$$
    $$15 = 3 \times 5$$
    $$\text{LCM } (12, 15) = 2 \times 2 \times 3 \times 5 = 60$$

39. **(19)**

    $$n(A \cup B) = n(A) + n(B) - n(A \cap B)$$
    $$= 10 + 12 - 3$$
    $$= 19$$

40. **(E)**

$\lvert 3x - 2 \rvert = 7$		$3x - 2 = -7$
$3x - 2 = 7$	or	$3x = -5$
$3x = 9$		$x = -\dfrac{5}{3}$
$x = 3$		

    Therefore, the solution set is $\{3, -\dfrac{5}{3}\}$.

41. **(D)** Let x = Number of hours it would take the mechanic working alone.

    Then $3x$ = Number of hours it would take the helper working alone. The relationship used in setting up the equation is:

$$\frac{1 \text{ job}}{x \text{ hrs.}} + \frac{1 \text{ job}}{3x \text{ hrs.}} = \frac{1 \text{ job}}{8 \text{ hrs.}} \text{ or, algebraically,}$$

$$\frac{1}{x} + \frac{1}{3x} = \frac{1}{8}$$

$$x = 10\frac{2}{3} \text{ hours by mechanic}$$

$$3x = 32 \text{ hours by helper}$$

Check:

$$\frac{8}{10\frac{2}{3}} + \frac{8}{32} = 1$$

$$\frac{24}{32} + \frac{1}{4} = 1$$

$$\frac{3}{4} + \frac{1}{4} = 1$$

42. **(D)**

$$\begin{cases} 3x + 4y = -6 & (1) \\ 5x + 6y = -8 & (2) \end{cases}$$

Multiply equation (1) by 3 and equation (2) by 2. Subtract equation (2) from equation (1):

$$9x + 12y = -18$$
$$-(10x + 12y = -16)$$
$$\overline{-x = -2}$$
$$x = 2$$

Substitute $x = 2$ into equation (1):

$$3(2) + 4y = -6$$

$$4y = -12$$

$$y = -3$$

Therefore, the solution set is $\{(2, -3)\}$.

43. **(A)**

$$\frac{7}{x+4} = \frac{5}{x+6}$$

Cross multiplying:

$$7x + 42 = 5x + 20$$

$$2x = -22$$

$$x = -11$$

44. **(D)**

$$\log_2 (x - 1) + \log_2 (x + 1) = 3$$

$$\log_2 (x - 1) (x + 1) = 3$$

$$(x - 1) (x + 1) = 2^3$$

$$x^2 - 1 = 8$$

$$x^2 = 9$$

$$x = 3$$

45. **(C)**   Because $10 < 31.4 < 100$, we must have $1 < x < 2$. Hence, without a calculator, and assuming one of the given answers is correct, we determine that (C) 1.50 is the correct answer.

46. **(29)**

$$f(3) = 3(3)^2 - (3) + 5$$

$$= 27 - 3 + 5$$

$$= 29$$

47. **(C)**

$$(-4) (-6) < xy < (-9) (-12)$$

$$24 < xy < 108$$

48. **(B)**

Distance = (rate) $\times$ (time).

Let x = time (hours) for second car to overtake first.

Distance of second car in x hours = $60x$.

Distance of first car in x hours = $40x$.

Since the second car has to travel 5 more miles, we have:

$$40x + 5 = 60x$$

or $\qquad 20x = 5 \Rightarrow x = \dfrac{1}{4}$hr.

49. **(D)**

$$\sqrt{108} + 3\sqrt{12} - 7\sqrt{3} = \sqrt{(36)(3)} + 3\sqrt{(4)(3)} = 7\sqrt{2}$$
$$= 6\sqrt{3} + 3\left(2\sqrt{3}\right) - 7\sqrt{3}$$
$$= 6\sqrt{3} + 6\sqrt{3} - 7\sqrt{3}$$
$$= 5\sqrt{3}.$$

50. **(A)**

$$\begin{cases} x - 3y = 1 \\ 2x + y = 2 \end{cases} \qquad\qquad\qquad (1) \\ (2)$$

Multiply equation (2) by 3. Add equation (2) to equation (1):

$$(1) + 3(2) \qquad x - 3y = 1$$
$$\underline{(+)\ 6x + 3y = 6}$$
$$7x + 0y = 7$$
$$x = 1$$

Substitute $x = 1$ into equation (1) $\rightarrow y = 0$. Therefore, the solution is $x = 1$ and $y = 0$.

51. **(D)**

 I. The sum of two positive integers is always a positive integer. Therefore, $x + y$ is a positive integer.

 II. If x is less than y, then $x - y$ is negative.

 III. The product of two positive integers is always a positive integer.

52. **(16)**

$$\log_8 x = \frac{4}{3}$$

$$x = (8)^{4/3}$$

$$x = [(8)^{1/3}]^4$$

$$x = [2]^4$$

$$x = 16$$

53. **(C)**   If $|x^2 - 3| < 1$, we have two possibilities:

$$|x^2 - 3| = (x^2 - 3) \text{ or} - (x^2 - 3)$$

a) $x^2 - 3 < 1$

$x^2 - 4 < 0$

$-2 < x < 2$

b) $-(x^2 - 3) < 1$

$-x^2 + 3 < 1$

$-x^2 + 2 < 0$

$x^2 - 2 > 0$

$x < -\sqrt{2} \text{ or } x > \sqrt{2}$

The solution can be represented graphically as shown below:

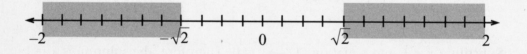

54. **(E)**

Let $y = \log_8 3 = x \log_2 3$.

Then $8^y = 3 \Rightarrow 2^{3y} = 3$ (1)

and $y = x\log_2 3 \Rightarrow 2^y = 3^x$ (2)

Substituting the expression for 2^y in equation (2) into (1), we obtain:

$$3 = (2^y)^3 = (3^x)^3 = 3^{3x}.$$

Hence, $3x = 1 \Rightarrow x = \dfrac{1}{3}.$

55. **(48)** Since Sir Lancelot must sit in an assigned chair and Sir Gawain on either side of him, there are 4! or 24 ways of seating the other 4. For each of these combinations, Sir Gawain can be in either of two seats, so the total number of ways of seating the knights is 24×2 or 48.

56. **(D)** Simplify:

$$\log_3(81)^{-2.3} = -2.3\log_3 3^4$$
$$= -2.3 \times 4\log_3 3$$
$$= -2.3 \times 4$$
$$= -9.2$$

57. **(D)** The expression

$$\log_2 \frac{\sqrt{2}}{8}$$

can be rewritten as:

$$\log_2 \frac{2^{1/2}}{2^3}$$

and by subtracting the exponents:

$$\log_2 2^{1/2-3} = \log_2 2^{-5/2} = \frac{-5}{2}$$

58. **(E)** The following formula can be used to solve this problem:

$$L = \sqrt{3^2 + 4^2 + 5^2}$$

Using your calculator, you can easily find the answer to be 7.07.

59. **(B)** A slope of a line is defined as the change rate of y with respect to x. By changing a line equation into the standard form, i.e., the form

$$y = ax + b,$$

you find the slope of the line easily, because it is simply a. Thus, for the given problem:

$$y = -\frac{15}{37}x + \frac{23}{37} = -0.405x + 0.623$$

So, $a = -0.405$.

60. **(D)** We employ the slope intercept form for the equation to be written, since we are given the y-intercept. Our task is then to determine the slope.

We are given the equation of a line parallel to the line whose equation we wish to find. We know that the slopes of two parallel lines are equal. Hence, by finding the slope of the given line, we will also be finding the unknown slope. To find the slope of the given equation

$$6x + 3y = 4$$

we transform the equation $6x + 3y = 4$ into slope intercept form.

$$6x + 3y = 4$$

$$3y = -6x + 4$$

$$y = -\frac{6}{3}x + \frac{4}{3}$$

$$y = -2x + \frac{4}{3}$$

Therefore, the slope of the line we are looking for is –2. The y-intercept is – 6. Applying the slope intercept form,

$$y = mx + b,$$

to the unknown line, we obtain,

$$y = -2x - 6$$

as the equation of the line.

61. **(A)**

$$\frac{\sqrt[3]{-16}}{\sqrt[3]{-2}} = \frac{\sqrt[3]{(-2)8}}{\sqrt[3]{-2}}$$

$$= \frac{\sqrt[3]{-2}\sqrt[3]{8}}{\sqrt[3]{-2}}$$

$$= \sqrt[3]{8} = 2$$

Note that since 3 is an odd number, $\sqrt[3]{-2}$ is defined to be a real number and is not imaginary.

62. **(B)** Let x = number of miles per hour in the rate of the head wind. Then since the head wind is detracting from the speed of the airplane, let

$300 - x$ = number of miles per hour in the ground speed of the airplane.

Applying the formula Rate × Time = Distance with rate = $(300 - x)$, Time = 4, and Distance = 900, we obtain:

$$(300 - x)(4) = 900$$

$$1{,}200 - 4x = 900$$

$$-4x = -300$$

$$x = 75$$

number of miles per hour in the rate of the head wind.

63. **(C)**

$$(f \circ g)(x) = f(x) \circ g(x) = f(g(x))$$

This is the definition of the composition of functions. For the functions given in this problem, we have

$$2(g(x)) + 4 = 2(x^2 - 2) + 4$$

$$= 2x^2 - 4 + 4 = 2x^2$$

64. **(C)** Note that

$$32 = 2 \times 2 \times 2 \times 2 \times 2 = 2^5.$$

Thus, $\log_{10}32 = \log_{10}2^5$.

Recall the logarithmic property,

$$\log_b x^y = y\log_b x.$$

Hence:

$$\log_{10} 32 = \log_{10} 2^5 = 5\log_{10} 2$$
$$= 5(0.3010)$$
$$= 1.5050$$

65. **(B)**

$$f(x) = x - 2x^2 + 2.$$

Therefore,

$$f(a-2) = (a-2) - 2(a-2)^2 + 2$$
$$= (a-2) - 2(a^2 - 4a + 4) + 2$$
$$= a - 2 - 2a^2 + 8a - 8 + 2$$
$$= 9a - 2a^2 - 8$$

66. **(A)** If $x^2 + bx + c = 0$, then by the quadratic formula

$$x = \frac{-b \pm \sqrt{b^2 - 4c}}{2}.$$

We are given $b^2 - 4c = 0$, so the two roots are

$$x_1 = \frac{-b+0}{2} \text{ and } x_2 = \frac{-b-0}{2}.$$

So x_1 and x_2 are real numbers and $x_1 = x_2$.

67. **(8)** "Total surface area is 24" implies that the area of one face is

$$\frac{24}{6} = 4 \text{ cm}^2.$$

Hence, the length of one side is 2 cm which implies the volume is

$$2^3 = 8 \text{ cm}^3.$$

68. **(A)**   First, calculate $g(2)$:

$$g(2) = 2^3 + 2 = 8 + 2 = 10$$

Thus, $f(g(2)) = f(10) = \sqrt{10+1} = \sqrt{11} = 3.3166$

69. **(A)**

$$\lim_{x\to 0}\left(\frac{x^2-2x}{x}\right) = \lim_{x\to 0}\left(\frac{x^2}{x} - \frac{2x}{x}\right)$$
$$= \lim_{x\to 0}(x-2)$$
$$= 0 - 2 = -2$$

Note that we could not set $x = 0$ before simplifying the fraction.

70. **(B)**

$$f(x) = 3x - 5 \text{ and } g(f(x)) = x$$

We want to know what value of x (in terms of x) would cause $g(3x - 5)$ to equal x. To distinguish one x from the other, we can represent the x from $3x - 5$ with a y. This will result in:

$$3y - 5 = x$$
$$3y = x + 5$$
$$y = \frac{x+5}{3}$$

$$g(y) = g(3x - 5) = \frac{3x - 5 + 5}{3} = x$$

PRACTICE
TEST 2

CLEP COLLEGE ALGEBRA
Practice Test 2

(Answer sheets appear in the back of this book.)

TIME: 90 Minutes
70 Questions

DIRECTIONS: Solve each problem, using any available space on the page for scratch work. Then either enter the correct numerical answer in the box provided, or decide which answer choice is the best and fill in the corresponding oval on the answer sheet.

NOTES:

(1) Unless otherwise specified, the domain of any function f is assumed to be the set of all real numbers x for which $f(x)$ is a real number.

(2) i will be used to denote $\sqrt{-1}$.

(3) All figures lie in a plane and are drawn to scale unless otherwise indicated.

---

1.   Find $2^{3/4} + 2^{4/3}$.

    (A) 4.2   (D) 6

    (B) 1.414   (E) 2.3

    (C) 8.5

2.   If f is defined by

$$f(x) = \frac{5x - 8}{2}$$

for each real number x, find the solution set for $f(x) > 2x$.

    (A) $\{x \mid x > 6\}$ (D) $\{x \mid 6 < x < 8\}$

    (B) $\{x \mid x > 8\}$ (E) None of the above.

    (C) $\{x \mid x < 8\}$

3. The function f is defined by

$$f(x) = \frac{1}{1+x}.$$

For what values of x is $f(f(x))$ undefined?

(A) $\{0\}$

(D) $\{-1, -\frac{1}{2}\}$

(B) $\{-1, 0\}$

(E) $\{-1, -2\}$

(C) $\{-\frac{1}{2}, 0\}$

4. If $f(x, y) = \dfrac{\log y}{\log x}$, then $f(4, 2) =$

(A) 0.

(D) 2.

(B) $\dfrac{1}{2}.$

(E) log2.

(C) 1.

5. Let $f : R \to R$ and $g : R \to R$ be two functions given by

$$f(x) = 2x + 5 \text{ and } g(x) = 4x^2$$

respectively for all x in R, where R is the set of real numbers. Find expressions for the composition $(f \circ g)(x)$.

(A) $8x^3 + 20x^2$

(D) $8x^3 + 5$

(B) $4(2x + 5)^2$

(E) None of the above.

(C) $8x^2 + 5$

6. A telephone number consists of seven digits. How many different telephone numbers exist if each digit appears only one time in the number?

(A) 7!

(D) 7^7

(B) 10^7

(E) $\dfrac{10!}{3!}$

(C) 70

7. $\log_3\left(\dfrac{1}{27}\right) =$

   (A) -3 (D) 3

   (B) $-\dfrac{1}{3}$ (E) 9

   (C) $\dfrac{1}{3}$

8. Simplify $\dfrac{\sqrt{-20}}{\sqrt{-5}}$.

   (A) $i\sqrt{4}$ (D) 2

   (B) $\sqrt{2}i$ (E) $\dfrac{i}{\sqrt{2}}$

   (C) $\dfrac{\sqrt{4}}{\sqrt{5}}i$

9. Which of the following is a root for the equation
   $-2x^2 + 4x + 5 = 0$?

   (A) 2.15 (D) 5.2

   (B) 3.48 (E) 3.22

   (C) 2.87

10. In the function

    $$f(x) = \dfrac{2x^2 + 3x + 5}{x^2 - 5x + 5}$$

    x cannot be

    (A) 3.62 and 1.38. (D) 3.15 and 6.24.

    (B) 0.25 and 1.37. (E) 10.2 and 2.3.

    (C) 5.2 and -7.8.

11. Jack is five times as old as Bill. Ten years from now, Jack will be at least three times as old as Bill will be then. At least how old is Jack now?

(A) 10 years   (D) 20 years

(B) 50 years   (E) 25 years

(C) 30 years

12. $t = -9$ is a root of the equation $t^2 + 4t - 45$. Which of the following statements is (are) correct for the equation?

   I. $t - 9$ is a factor of the equation.

   II.   Division of the equation by $t - 9$ yields the other factor of the quadratic equation.

   III. $t = -5$ is another root of the equation.

(A) I only.   (D) I, II, and III.

(B) II and III only.   (E) None of the statements are correct.

(C) III only.

13. If $f(x) = 2^x + 4$ and $g(x) = \dfrac{1}{x}$, then $f(g(f(x)))$ is

(A) $\dfrac{1}{2^x + 4}.$ (D) $^{(2x+4)}\sqrt{2} + 4.$

(B) $2^{\frac{1}{x}} + 4.$ (E) $\dfrac{1}{2^{2x}} + 4.$

(C) $\dfrac{1}{2^{x+4}}.$

14. Obtain the equation of the line passing through point $P(-1, -3)$ and with an inclination of $45°$.

(A) $y = x + 2$ (D) $y = x + 1$

(B) $y = x + 4$ (E) $y = x - 2$

(C) $y = -x + 4$

15. A cube has its length, width, and height all equal to 5. The length of its diagonal is

(A) 11.2.

(D) 9.1.

(B) 5.22.

(E) 7.2.

(C) 8.66.

16. Simplify the expression $\dfrac{4! + 3!}{5!}$.

(A) $\dfrac{3}{10}$

(D) $\dfrac{3}{20}$

(B) $\dfrac{1}{5}$

(E) $\dfrac{12}{5}$

(C) $\dfrac{1}{4}$

17. If $f(x) = x^3 + 2x - 1$, then $f(2 - a) =$

(A) $8 - 8a + 2a^2 - 4a - 1$

(D) $14a + 8 - 6a^2 + a^3$

(B) $8 - 8a - 4a + a^3 - 1$

(E) Cannot be determined.

(C) $11 - 14a + 6a^2 - a^3$

18. Consider the function

$f(x) = x^3 + 3x - k.$

If $f(2) = 10$, then $k =$

(A) 4.

(D) 18.

(B) –4.

(E) 14.

(C) 0.

19. Find the smallest of three consecutive positive integers such that when five times the largest is subtracted from the square of the middle one, the result exceeds three times the smallest by 7.

⬚

20. Five consulting firms agree to contribute equally to the cost of a joint technical library. If three more firms join the plan, the cost to each member of the group would be reduced by $900. Find the cost of the library.

    (A) $9,000   (D) $18,000

    (B) $12,000   (E) $4,500

    (C) $6,000

21. Solve for x, when $|5 - 3x| = -2$.

    (A) $\dfrac{7}{3}$ (D) 1

    (B) $-\dfrac{7}{3}$ (E) No solution.

    (C) -1

22. The solution set for

    $$\frac{x^2 - 5x + 6}{x - 2} > 0$$

    is

    (A) $\{x \mid x < 3\}$.   (D) $\{x \mid 2 < x < 3\}$.

    (B) $\{x \mid 2 < x < 3 \text{ or } x < -2\}$.   (E) $\{x \mid x > 3\}$.

    (C) $\{x \mid -2 < x < 3\}$.

23. What is the domain of the function defined by

    $y = f(x) = \sqrt{-x+1} + 5$?

    (A) $\{x \mid x \geq 0\}$ (D) $\{x \mid x \geq -1\}$

    (B) $\{x \mid x \leq 1\}$ (E) $\{x \mid x \leq -1\}$

    (C) $\{x \mid 0 \leq x \leq 1\}$

24. What is the range of the function given in the previous question?

    (A) $\{y \mid y \geq 5\}$ (D) $\{y \mid 0 < y \leq 5\}$

    (B) $\{y \mid y > 5\}$ (E) $\{$ all real numbers $\}$

    (C) $\{y \mid y > 0\}$

25. If $f(x) = \dfrac{x-1}{x^3 - 3x^2 + 2x}$, for what value(s) of x is $f(x)$ undefined?

(A) 0

(D) 0, 1, and 2

(B) 0 and 2

(E) 0, –1, and –2

(C) 1 and 2

26. If a straight line contains points (3, 4) and (–2, 7), then the equation of this straight line is

(A) $y = -\dfrac{3}{5}x + \dfrac{29}{5}$.

(D) $y = \dfrac{4}{3}x + \dfrac{7}{3}$.

(B) $y = -\dfrac{11}{5}x - \dfrac{29}{5}$.

(E) $y = -\dfrac{2}{7}x + \dfrac{29}{7}$.

(C) $y = -\dfrac{5}{3}x + \dfrac{29}{3}$.

27. If $f(x) = \sqrt{x}$, $g(x) = \dfrac{x-1}{4}$, and $h(x) = x^2$, what is $f(g(h(4)))$?

(A) 2

(D) 1.94

(B) 2.06

(E) 3.75

(C) 2.24

28. If $f(x) = x^3 - x - 1$, then the set of all c for which $f(c) = f(-c)$ is

(A) {all real numbers}.

(D) { – 1, 0, 1 }.

(B) { 0 }.

(E) ϕ.

(C) { 0, 1 }.

29. If $f(x) = (x - 1)^2 + (x + 1)^2$ for all real numbers x, which of the following are true?

  I. $f(x) = f(-x)$

  II. $f(x) = f(x + 1)$

  III. $f(x) = |f(x)|$

(A) None of these.   (D) II and III only.

(B) III only.   (E) I, II, and III.

(C) I and III only.

30. If $f(x) = -x^3 - 2x^2 + 4x - 8$, what is $f(-2x)$?

(A) $8x^3 - 8x^2 - 8x - 8$ (D) $-8x^3 - 4x^2 - 8x - 8$

(B) $-8x^3 + 8x^2 - 8x - 8$ (E) $8x^3 - 6x^2 - 6x - 8$

(C) $8x^3 - 4x^2 - 8x - 8$

31. If the sum of three consecutive odd numbers is 51, what is the first odd number of the sequence?

32. If $x = \sqrt{3}$ and $y = \sqrt{2}$, then $(2x + 3y)(x + y) =$

(A) $6 + \sqrt{6}$.   (D) $10 + 5\sqrt{6}$.

(B) $6 + 3\sqrt{6}$.   (E) $12 + 5\sqrt{6}$.

(C) $9 + 2\sqrt{6}$.

33. If $2^{3x} = 64$, then $x =$

(A) 0.   (D) 3.

(B) 1.   (E) 4.

(C) 2.

34. If $f(x) = 2x + 1$ and $g(x) = 3x - 5$, what is $f(g(2))$?

35. If a line contains the points $(1, 3)$ and $(-2, -4)$, then its slope is

(A) 3.   (D) 1.

(B) $\dfrac{7}{3}$.   (E) $\dfrac{2}{3}$.

(C) $\dfrac{5}{3}$.

36. If $x^2 - 3x - 4 < 0$, then the solution set is

(A) $-4 < x < 1$.

(D) $-1 < x < 0$.

(B) $-4 < x < -3$.

(E) $-1 < x < 4$.

(C) $-3 < x < 0$.

37. If a and b are positive integers such that

$$c = 12a + 54b,$$

then c must be divisible by which of the following?

(A) 4

(D) 9

(B) 6

(E) 27

(C) 8

38. If $\log_3 (x + 7) = 2$, then $x =$

(A) -1.

(D) 4.

(B) 2.

(E) 6.

(C) 3.

39. If $x = 3 + 2i$ and $y = 1 + 3i$, where $i^2 = -1$, then $\dfrac{x}{y} =$

(A) $\dfrac{9}{10} - \dfrac{2}{3}i$.

(D) $3 - \dfrac{7}{10}i$.

(B) $\dfrac{9}{10} - \dfrac{7}{3}i$.

(E) $3 + \dfrac{2}{3}i$.

(C) $\dfrac{9}{10} + \dfrac{2}{3}i$.

40. If $x = (a - 3)^2$ and $a = -2$, what is the value of x?

$$\boxed{}$$

41. How many integers are in the solution set of $|3x - 2| > -1$?

(A) None

(D) Three

(B) One

(E) Infinitely many

(C) Two

42. If a line contains the points $(-2, 3)$ and $(4, -1)$, then its y-intercept is

(A) -3.

(D) $\dfrac{5}{3}$.

(B) $-\dfrac{2}{3}$.

(E) $\dfrac{5}{2}$.

(C) 0.

43. If $f(x) = 3x - 1$, then $f^{-1}(x) =$

(A) $3x + 1$.

(D) $\dfrac{1}{3}x + \dfrac{1}{3}$.

(B) $x - \dfrac{1}{3}$.

(E) $\dfrac{1}{3}x - 1$.

(C) $2x - 2$.

44. If $x + yi = (3 + 2i)(1 + 3i)$, and $i = \sqrt{-1}$, then $x =$

(A) -3.

(D) 6.

(B) -1.

(E) 9.

(C) 3.

45. If $\dfrac{2}{3}x = 1$, then $\dfrac{3}{4} + x =$

(A) $\dfrac{9}{4}$.

(D) 1.

(B) 2.

(E) $\dfrac{3}{4}$.

(C) $\dfrac{7}{4}$.

46. Find the coordinates of the intersection of the following two lines:

$x + 2y = 5$ and

$2x + 3y = 2$.

(A) $(-12, 6)$ (D) $(10, 10)$

(B) $(-11, 8)$ (E) $(11, 12)$

(C) $(-10, 9)$

47. How many integers are in the solution set of $|2x - 6| < 3$?

(A) None   (D) Three

(B) One   (E) Four

(C) Two

48. Four officers must be chosen from a high school committee of eight freshmen and five sophomores, with exactly two officers to be chosen from each class. In how many ways can these officers be chosen?

49. Add $(3 + 4i)$ and $(2 - 5i)$.

(A) $6 + 9i$ (D) $6 - i$

(B) $5 - i$ (E) $5 + 9i$

(C) $26 - 7i$

50. Subtract $7 - 2i$ from $-3 + 5i$.

(A) $10 - 7i$ (D) $-10 + 3i$

(B) $-11 + 41i$ (E) $-10 + 7i$

(C) $-5 + 2i$

51. Find the product $(2 + 3i)(-2 - 5i)$.

(A) $-11 + 16i$ (D) $11 + 4i$

(B) $-19 + 16i$ (E) $11 - 16i$

(C) -35

52. Without solving the equation, $2x^2 - 3x + 5 = 0$ has

(A) real and equal roots.

(B) real and unequal roots.

(C) imaginary roots.

(D) infinitely many roots.

(E) Cannot determine the nature of the roots.

53. Simplify $\dfrac{3 - 5i}{2 + 3i}$.

(A) $21 - i$

(B) $\dfrac{-9}{13} - \dfrac{19}{13}i$

(C) $\dfrac{21}{13} - \dfrac{1}{13}i$

(D) $-9 - 19i$

(E) Cannot be simplified.

54. Solve $|\, 3x - 1 \,| \leq 8$.

(A) $x \leq 3$

(B) $\dfrac{-7}{3} \leq x \leq 3$

(C) $-7 \leq x \leq 3$

(D) $x \leq \dfrac{8}{3}$

(E) $\dfrac{-7}{3} \leq x \leq 8$

55. Which of the following points $(1, 0)$, $(-1, 0)$, $(4, 4)$, and $(9, 17)$ belong to the graph of the equation $y = x^{3/2} - x$?

(A) $(1, 0)$

(B) $(-1, 0)$

(C) $(4, 4)$

(D) $(9, 7)$

(E) $(1, 0)$ and $(4, 4)$

56. Find the next three terms of the geometric progression

$1, 2, 4, 8, \dots$

(A) 12, 20, and 32

(B) 16, 32, and 64

(C) 16, 20, and 24

(D) 16, 18, and 20

(E) 1, 2, and 4

57. Find the sum of the first 20 terms of the arithmetic progression

$-9, -3, 3, \ldots$

58. A table tennis tournament is to be round-robin; that is, each player plays one match against every other player. The winner of the tournament is determined by the best scores in the matches. How many matches will be played if five people enter the tournament?

59. Find the zeros of the function

$$\frac{2x+7}{5} + \frac{3x-5}{4} + \frac{33}{10}.$$

(A) -3 (D) -7

(B) 7 (E) 3

(C) -5

60. Expand $(2 + 3i)^3$.

(A) $46 - 9i$ (D) $8 - 27i$

(B) $-46 + 9i$ (E) $26 + 9i$

(C) $-18i$

TEST STOPS HERE. *EXTRA PRACTICE FOLLOWS...*

61. Solve the equation $\sqrt{x^2 - 3x} = 2x - 6$.

(A) $\dfrac{-3 + 3\sqrt{65}}{8}$ and $\dfrac{-3 - 3\sqrt{65}}{8}$

(B) -6 and 1

(C) -3 and -4

(D) -1 and 6

(E) 3 and 4

62. Find the equation of the line that passes through (3, 2) and is perpendicular to

$$x + 3y - 6 = 0.$$

(A) $3x - y - 11 = 0$ (D) $3x + y - 11 = 0$

(B) $3x - y - 7 = 0$ (E) $x + 3y + 3 = 0$

(C) $x - 3y - 9 = 0$

63. Find the equation for the circle whose center is at the origin and whose radius is 3.

(A) $x^2 + y^2 = 9$ (D) $x^2 + y^2 = 3$

(B) $x^2 + y^2 - 6x - 6y = 18$ (E) $x^2 + y^2 - 6x - 6y = -18$

(C) $x^2 + y^2 + 6x - 6y = 0$

64. In a class of 20 students a student either speaks German or Chinese or both. Thirteen students speak German and 17 speak Chinese. How many speak both German and Chinese?

> [   ]

65. Solve $A = \dfrac{h}{2}(b + B)$ for h.

(A) $2A - b - B$ (D) $\dfrac{2A}{b + B}$

(B) $\dfrac{A}{2(b + B)}$ (E) $\dfrac{2A}{bB}$

(C) $2A(b + B)$

66. Determine the quadratic equation whose roots are

$$x = 2 + \sqrt{3} \text{ and } x = 2 - \sqrt{3}.$$

(A) $x^2 + 2x - 3 = 0$ (D) $x^2 + 3x + 2 = 0$

(B) $x^2 - 4x + 1 = 0$ (E) $x^2 + 4x - 9 = 0$

(C) $x^2 - 12 = 0$

67. Find the real numbers a and b such that

$$(a + bi) + (2 - 3i) = 2\,(-2 + i).$$

(A) $a = -2$ and $b = -2$ (D) $a = -6$ and $b = 5$

(B) $a = 5$ and $b = -6$ (E) $a = -6$ and $b = -1$

(C) $a = -2$ and $b = 16$

68. Determine the constant A so that the lines $3x - 4y = 12$ and $Ax + 6y = -9$ are parallel.

(A) $\dfrac{-9}{2}$ (D) 8

(B) $\dfrac{3}{4}$ (E) $\dfrac{-3}{4}$

(C) $\dfrac{4}{3}$

69. Find the value of $3x^2 - 4x - 2$, for

$$x = \frac{2 - \sqrt{10}}{3}.$$

(A) $\dfrac{-20 + 4\sqrt{10}}{3}$ (D) $-8 + 3\sqrt{10}$

(B) 90 (E) 0

(C) $2 - \sqrt{10}$

70. Find the equation of the tangent to the parabola

$$y = x^2 - 6x + 9,$$

if the slope of the tangent line equals 2.

(A) $y = -7x + 2$ (D) $y = 2x - 7$

(B) $y = 2x + 25$ (E) $y = 2x + 7$

(C) $y = 2x - 25$

CLEP COLLEGE ALGEBRA
TEST 2

ANSWER KEY

1. (A)	19. (8)	37. (B)	55. (E)
2. (B)	20. (B)	38. (B)	56. (B)
3. (E)	21. (E)	39. (B)	57. (960)
4. (D)	22. (E)	40. (25)	58. (10)
5. (C)	23. (B)	41. (E)	59. (A)
6. (E)	24. (A)	42. (D)	60. (B)
7. (A)	25. (B)	43. (D)	61. (E)
8. (D)	26. (A)	44. (A)	62. (B)
9. (C)	27. (D)	45. (A)	63. (A)
10. (A)	28. (D)	46. (B)	64. (10)
11. (B)	29. (C)	47. (D)	65. (D)
12. (E)	30. (A)	48. (1,120)	66. (B)
13. (D)	31. (15)	49. (B)	67. (D)
14. (E)	32. (E)	50. (E)	68. (A)
15. (C)	33. (C)	51. (E)	69. (E)
16. (C)	34. (3)	52. (C)	70. (D)
17. (C)	35. (B)	53. (B)	
18. (A)	36. (E)	54. (B)	

DETAILED EXPLANATIONS
OF ANSWERS

TEST 2

1. **(A)**   Simplifying power terms into more familiar form is the first step for this problem. This is done like this:

$$x^{\frac{q}{p}} = \sqrt[p]{x^q}$$

So, the problem can be put into a simpler form of the following:

$$\sqrt[3]{2^4} + \sqrt[4]{2^3} = \sqrt[3]{16} + \sqrt[4]{8}$$

which equals 4.2.

2. **(B)**   To find the solution set of $f(x) > 2x$, we proceed as follows:

$$\frac{5x-8}{2} > 2x$$

$$5x - 8 > 4x$$

which implies $x > 8$.

3. **(E)**

$$f(f(x)) = \cfrac{1}{1 + \cfrac{1}{1 = x}},$$

which is undefined for

$$1 + x = 0 \text{ and } 1 + \frac{1}{1 = x} = 0.$$

That is, $f(f(x))$ is undefined for $x = -1$ and $x = -2$.

4. **(D)**

$$f(4,2) = \frac{\log 4}{\log 2} = \frac{\log 2^2}{\log 2} = \frac{2\log 2}{\log 2} = 2$$

5. **(C)** Consider functions $f: A \to B$ and $g: B \to C$, that is, where the codomain of f is the domain of g. Then the function $g \circ f$ is defined as $g \circ f: A \to C$ where

$$(g \circ f)(x) = g(f(x))$$

for all x in A, and it is called the composition of f and g.

In another notation,

$$g \circ f = \{(x, z) \in A \times C \mid \text{for all } y \in B$$

such that $\quad (x, y) \in f$ and $(y, z) \in g\}$.

So $\quad (f \circ g)(x) = f(g(x))$

$$= f(4x + 2)$$

$$= 2(4x^2) + 5$$

$$= 8x^2 + 5$$

6. **(E)** There are 10 integers from 0 to 9; hence, there are 10 choices for the first digit of the phone number. Since no digit can be repeated, we have only nine choices for the second digit. Similarly, there are eight choices for the third digit and so on. Since there are seven digits in a phone number, we have

$$10 \times 9 \times 8 \times 7 \times 6 \times 5 \times 4 = \frac{10!}{3!}$$

possible phone numbers.

7. **(A)**

$$\log_3\left(\frac{1}{27}\right) = \log_3\left(\frac{1}{3^3}\right) = \log(3^{-3}) = -3$$

We could also use the identity:

$$\log_a b^c = c\log_a b$$

and write:

$$\log_3 \frac{1}{27} = \log_3 3^{-3} = -3\log_3 3 = -3$$

8. **(D)**

$$\frac{\sqrt{-20}}{\sqrt{-5}} = \frac{i\sqrt{20}}{i\sqrt{5}} = \frac{\sqrt{4}\sqrt{5}}{\sqrt{5}} = \sqrt{4} = 2$$

9. **(C)** This is a typical second order equation, so the formula

$$r_{1,2} = \frac{-b \pm \sqrt{b^2 - 4ac}}{2a}$$

can be used. The two roots are 2.87 and –0.87.

10. **(A)** The domain of this function is constrained to x that does not make $f(x)$ become infinite, in which case we say the function is defined on that domain. The values of x that can make the function undefined are the roots of the denominator,

$$x^2 - 5x + 5.$$

Using the following formula, you can find these roots:

$$r_{1,2} = \frac{-b \pm \sqrt{b^2 - 4ac}}{2a}$$

Since here $a = 1$, $b = -5$, and $c = 5$, you can easily find these roots to be 3.62 and 1.38.

11. **(B)** Let J and B represent Jack's and Bill's ages respectively. We know that Jack is five times as old as Bill and can therefore conclude: $J = 5B$.

We also know that in 10 years Jack will be $J + 10$ years old and Bill will be $B + 10$ years old. At that time, Jack will be at least three times as old as Bill. So $(J + 10) \geq 3(B + 10)$.

We know $J = 5B$ and may therefore substitute this value into the second equation to obtain:

$$((5B) + 10) \geq 3B + 30$$

$$2B \geq 20$$

$$B \geq 10$$

Bill is at least 10 years old now, so Jack must be at least 50 years old.

12. **(E)** Since $t = -9$ is a root of the equation

$$t^2 + 4t - 45,$$

then $(t + 9)$ is a factor. Division of the equation by $(t + 9)$ would therefore yield the other factor of the quadratic, which is $(t - 5)$, giving the second root, $t = 5$.

13. **(D)**

$$f(g(f(x))) = f(z), \text{ where } z = g(f(x))$$

$$g(f(x)) = g(w), \text{ where } w = f(x)$$

$$w = f(x) = 2^x + 4$$

$$g(w) = \frac{1}{w} = \frac{1}{2^x + 4} = g(f(x))$$

$$f(z) = 2^z + 4, \text{ but } z = g(f(x)) = \frac{1}{2^x + 4}$$

$$f(z) = 2^{\frac{1}{2x+4}} + 4 = {}^{(2x+4)}\!\sqrt{2} + 4$$

14. **(E)** A line with an inclination of $45°$ has a slope m which is equal to $\tan 45°$. The equation of a line can be written as shown:

$$y - y_0 = m (x - x_0)$$

The ordered pair (x_0, y_0) is given and $m = \tan 45° = 1$. By substitution we obtain:

$$(y - (-3)) = 1(x - (-1))$$

$$y + 3 = x + 1$$

$$y = x - 2$$

15. **(C)** As shown in the figure, the diagonal on each side of the cube is

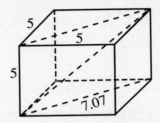

$$\sqrt{5^2 + 5^2} = 7.07$$

The diagonal of the cube lies in the rectangle whose height is 5 and width is 7.07, as shown in the figure. Therefore, it can be easily found that the length of the diagonal is

$$\sqrt{5^2 + 7.07^2} = 8.66$$

16. **(C)**

$$\frac{4! + 3!}{5!} = \frac{(4)3! + 3!}{(5)(4)\,3!} = \frac{(4+1)3!}{(5)(4)\,3!}$$

$$= \frac{4+1}{(5)4} = \frac{5}{20} = \frac{1}{4}$$

17. **(C)**

$$f(x) = x^3 + 2x - 1$$

$$\therefore \quad f(2-a) = (2-a)^3 + 2(2-a) - 1$$

$$= (8 - 8a + 2a^2 - 4a + 4a^2 - a^3) + (4 - 2a) - 1$$

$$= 11 - 14a + 6a^2 - a^3$$

18. **(A)**

$$f(x) = x^3 + 3x - k$$

since $\quad f(2) = 10,$

we have $\quad 10 = (2)^3 + 3(2) - k,$

or $\quad 10 = 8 + 6 - 8 \Rightarrow k = 4.$

19. **(8)** Let x be the smallest number; this implies that the three consecutive numbers are x, $x + 1$, and $x + 2$. Therefore,

$$(x + 1)^2 - 5(x + 2) = 3x + 7$$

$$x^2 + 2x + 1 - 5x - 10 = 3x + 7$$

which leads to

$$x^2 - 6x - 16 = 0$$

or $\quad (x - 8)(x + 2) = 0$

$\Rightarrow \qquad\qquad x = -2 \text{ or } 8.$

But x cannot be a negative integer, so $x = 8$ is the answer.

20. **(B)** Let x be the cost of the library. When five firms are involved, $1/_5x$ is the cost each firm will bear. When eight firms are involved $1/_8x$ will be each firm's share. Since we are told that the latter share is \$900 less than the former, then

$$\frac{1}{8}x = \frac{1}{5}x - 900.$$

Solving, we find that x, the cost of the library, is

$$\frac{3}{40}x = 900.$$

$$x = \frac{300 \times 40}{1} = \$12,000$$

21. **(E)** This problem has no solution, since the absolute value can never be negative.

22. **(E)**

$$\frac{x^2 - 5x + 6}{x - 2} = \frac{(x - 3)(x - 2)}{x - 2} = x - 3 > 0$$

$x > 3$

23. **(B)** The only restriction for the domain is that $-x + 1$ must be greater than or equal to zero.

$$-x + 1 \geq 0$$

$$\Rightarrow x \leq 1$$

24. **(A)**

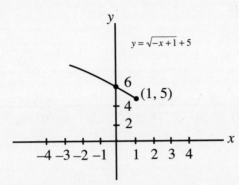

Since $\sqrt{-x+1} \geq 0$, the range is all values of $y \geq 5$.

25. **(B)**

$$f(x) = \frac{x-1}{x^3 - 3x^2 + 2}$$

$$= \frac{x-1}{x(x^2 - 3x + 2)}$$

$$= \frac{x-1}{x(x-1)(x-2)}$$

$$= \frac{1}{x(x-2)}$$

$f(x)$ is undefined when $x(x - 2) = 0$, or $x = 0$ and $x = 2$.

The factors of $x^2 - 3x + 2$ can be calculated by using the quadratic formula:

$$x = \frac{-1(-3) \pm \sqrt{9 - 4 \times 1 \times 2}}{2} = \frac{3 \pm 1}{2}$$

$$(3 + 1) \div 2 = 2$$

$$(3 - 1) \div 2 = 1$$

Therefore, the factors are $(x - 2)$ and $(x - 1)$.

26. **(A)**   The equation of a straight line with slope m and y-intercept c is given by:

$$y = mx + c$$

slope: $m = \dfrac{7-4}{-2-3} = \dfrac{3}{-5} = -\dfrac{3}{5}$

Thus, $y = -\dfrac{3}{5}x + c$

Since points $(3, 4)$ and $(-2, 7)$ satisfy this equation,

$4 = -\dfrac{3}{5}(3) + c$

$c = 4 + \dfrac{9}{5} = \dfrac{29}{5}$

Thus, the equation of the line is

$y = -\dfrac{3}{5}x + \dfrac{29}{5}$

27. **(D)**

$h(4) = 4^2 = 16$

$g(h(4)) = \dfrac{16-1}{4} = \dfrac{15}{4} = 3.75$

$f(g(h(4))) = \sqrt{3.75} = 1.94$

28. **(D)**

$f(c) = c^3 - c - 1, f(-c) = -c^3 + c - 1$

$c^3 - c - 1 = c^3 + c - 1$

$c^3 = c$

$\therefore \qquad c = -1, 0,$ or 1

29. **(C)**

I.   True: $f(-x) = (-x-1)^2 + (-x+1)^2 = [-(x+1)]^2 + [-(x-1)]^2$

$= (x+1)^2 + (x-1)^2 = f(x)$

II.   False: $f(x+1) = (x+1-1)^2 + (x+1+1)^2$

$= x^2 (x+2)^2 \neq f(x)$

III.   True: $|f(x)| = |(x-1)^2 + (x+1)^2|$

$$= (x-1)^2 + (x+1)^2 = f(x)$$

30. **(A)**

$$f(-2x) = -(-2x)^3 - 2(-2x)^2 + 4(-2x) - 8$$

$$= -(-8x^3) - 2(4x^2) - 8x - 8$$

$$= 8x^3 - 8x^2 - 8x - 8$$

31. **(15)**   Let x be the first odd number. Then,

$$x + (x+2) + (x+4) = 51$$

$$3x + 6 = 51$$

$$3x = 45$$

$$x = 15$$

32. **(E)**

$$(2x + 3y)(x + y) = 2x^2 + 2xy + 3xy + 3y^2$$

$$= 2x^2 + 5xy + 3y^2$$

$$= 2(\sqrt{3})^2 + 5(\sqrt{3})(\sqrt{2}) + 3(\sqrt{2})^2$$

$$= 2(3) + 5\sqrt{6} + 3(2)$$

$$= 12 + 5\sqrt{6}$$

33. **(C)**

$$2^{3x} = 64$$

$$(2^3)^x = 64$$

$$8^x = 64$$

$$x = 2$$

34. **(3)**

$$f(g(2)) = f(3(2) - 5)$$

$$= f(1)$$

$$= 2(1) + 1$$
$$= 3$$

35. **(B)**

$$\text{slope} = \frac{y_2 - y_1}{x_2 - x_1} = \frac{3 - (-4)}{1 - (-2)} = \frac{7}{3}$$

36. **(E)**

$$x^2 - 3x - 4 < 0$$
$$(x + 1)(x - 4) < 0$$
$$-1 < x < 4$$

37. **(B)**

$$c = 12a + 54b$$
$$= 6(2a + 9b)$$

Therefore, c must be divisible by 6, the greatest common divisor of 12 and 54.

38. **(B)**

$$\log_3 (x + 7) = 2$$
$$x + 7 = 3^2$$
$$x + 7 = 9$$
$$x = 2$$

39. **(B)**

$$\frac{x}{y} = \frac{3 + 2i}{1 + 3i}$$
$$= \frac{3 + 2i}{1 + 3i} \times \frac{1 - 3i}{1 - 3i}$$
$$= \frac{3 - 9i + 2i - 6i^2}{1^2 - 3^2 i^2}$$

$$= \frac{9 - 7i}{1 + 9}$$

$$= \frac{9}{10} - \frac{7}{10}i$$

40. **(25)**

$$x = (a - 3)^2$$

$$= (-2 - 3)^2$$

$$= (-5)^2$$

$$= 25$$

41. **(E)** Since the absolute value of an expression is non-negative, it must be greater than -1. Therefore, the solution set is the entire real axis, which contains an infinite number of integers.

42. **(D)** Use the slope-y-intercept form of an equation which is given as $y - y_0 = m(x - x_0) + b$ where m is the slope, b is the y-intercept, and point (x_0, y_0) is a point on the line. The slope is given as

$$\frac{y_1 - y_0}{x_1 - x_0}.$$

Substituting, we obtain:

$$y - (-1) = \frac{3 - (-1)}{-2 - 4}(x - 4)$$

$$y + 1 = \frac{4}{-6}(x - 4)$$

$$y = \frac{-2}{3}x + \frac{9}{3} - 1$$

$$y = \frac{2}{3}x + \frac{5}{3}$$

The y-intercept is equal to b, which is $5/3$.

43. **(D)** To find the inverse of a function, we have to interchange x and y in the given equation and express the new y in terms of x.

$$f(x) = 3x - 1$$

$$y = 3x - 1$$

$$x = 3y - 1 \quad \text{(Interchange } x \text{ and } y\text{)}$$

$$3y = x + 1$$

$$y = \frac{1}{3}(x + 1)$$

$$y = \frac{1}{3}x + \frac{1}{3}$$

Check:

$$f^{-1}(f(x)) = f^{-1}(3x - 1)$$

$$= \frac{1}{3}(3x - 1) + \frac{1}{3}$$

$$= x - \frac{1}{3} + \frac{1}{3}$$

$$= x$$

44. **(A)**

$$(3 + 2i)(1 + 3i) = 3 + 9i + 2i + 6i^2$$

$$= -3 + 11i$$

Therefore, $x = -3$.

45. **(A)**

$$\frac{2}{3}x = 1$$

$$x = \frac{3}{2}$$

$$\frac{3}{4} + x = \frac{3}{4} + \frac{3}{2} = \frac{9}{4}$$

46. **(B)**

$$x + 2y = 5 \qquad (1)$$
$$2x + 3y = 2 \qquad (2)$$

Multiply equation (1) by 2 and subtract equation (2):

$$2x + 4y = 10$$
$$-(2x + 3y = 2)$$
$$y = 8$$

Substitute $y = 8$ into equation (1):

$$x + 2(8) = 5$$
$$x = -11$$

Therefore, $(-11, 8)$ is the intersection point of the given pair of lines.

47. **(D)**

$$|2x - 6| < 3$$
$$-3 < 2x - 6 < 3$$
$$3 < 2x < 9$$
$$1.5 < x < 4.5$$

Therefore, the solution set contains only three integers: 2, 3, and 4.

48. **(1,120)** There are:

8 choices for first freshman officer,

7 choices for second freshman officer,

5 for first sophomore officer,

and   4 for second sophomore officer.

Thus, $8 \times 7 \times 5 \times 4 = 1,120$.

49. **(B)**

$$(3 + 4i) + (2 - 5i) = 3 \neq 4i + 2 - 5i = 5 - i$$

50. **(E)**

$$(-3 + 5i) - (7 - 2i) = -3 + 5i - 7 + 2i = -10 + 7i$$

51. **(E)**

$$(2 + 3i)(-2 - 5i) = (2)(-2) + (2)(-5i) + (3i)(-2) + (3i)(-5i)$$

$$= -4 - 10i - 6i - 15i^2$$

$$= -4 - 16i - 15(-1)$$

$$= -4 - 16i + 15$$

$$= 11 - 16i$$

52. **(C)**

$$2x^2 - 3x + 5 = 0$$

$$a = 2 \quad b = -3 \quad c = 5$$

$$b^2 - 4ac = (-3)^2 - 4(2)(5)$$

$$= 9 - 40 = -31$$

Since the discriminant is negative, we know that the roots will be imaginary.

53. **(B)**

$$\frac{3 - 5i}{2 + 3i} = \frac{3 - 5i}{2 + 3i} \times \frac{2 - 3i}{2 - 3i}$$

$$= \frac{(3 - 5i)(2 - 3i)}{(2 + 3i)(2 - 3i)}$$

$$= \frac{6 - 9i - 10i + 15i^2}{4 - 6i + 6i - 9i^2}$$

$$= \frac{6 - 19i - 15}{4 + 9}$$

$$= \frac{-9 - 19i}{13} = \frac{-9}{13} - \frac{19}{13}i$$

54. **(B)**

$$|3x - 1| \le 8$$

$$-8 \le 3x - 1 \le 8$$

$$-7 \le 3x \le 9$$

$$\frac{-7}{3} \le x \le 3$$

55. **(E)**

$(1, 0)$ $y = x^{3/2} - x = (\sqrt{1})^3 - 1 = 1 - 1 = 0 = 0$

$(-1, 0)$ $y = x^{3/2} - x = (\sqrt{-1})^3 - (-1) = -i + 1 \ne 0$

$(4, 4)$ $y = x^{3/2} - x = (\sqrt{4})^3 - 4 = 8 - 4 = 4 = 4$

$(9, 17)$ $y = x^{3/2} - x = (\sqrt{9})^3 - 9 = 27 - 9 = 18 \ne 17$

Therefore, $(1, 0)$ and $(4, 4)$ belong to the graph.

56. **(B)** $1, 2, 4, 8, \ldots$

$$r = \frac{a_2}{a_1} = \frac{2}{1} = 2$$

$$a_n = a_1 r^{n-1} = (2)^{n-1}$$

$$a_5 = (2)^{5-1} = (2)^4 = 16$$

$$a_6 = (2)^{6-1} = (2)^5 = 32$$

$$a_7 = (2)^{7-1} = (2)^6 = 64$$

57. **(960)** $-9, -3, 3, \ldots$

$$d = a_2 - a_1 = -3 - (-9) = 6$$

$$a_n = a_1 + (n - 1)\, d$$

$$a_{20} = -9 + (20 - 1)(6)$$

$$= -9 + (19)(6) = -9 + 114 = 105$$

$$S_n = \frac{n}{2}(a_1 + a_{20})$$

$$S_{20} = \frac{20}{2}[-9 + 105] = 10[96] = 960$$

58. **(10)**   Label the players 1 through 5. Player 1 will have one match with each of the remaining four players. Player 2 (who has already played Player 1) will have matches with the remaining three players and so on. The total number of matches will be

$$4 + 3 + 2 + 1 = 10$$

59. **(A)**

$$\frac{2x + 7}{5} + \frac{3x - 5}{4} + \frac{33}{10} = 0$$

$$20\left(\frac{2x + 7}{5}\right) + 20\left(\frac{3x - 5}{4}\right) + 20\left(\frac{33}{10}\right) = 20(0)$$

$$4(2x + 7) + 5(3x - 5) + 2(33) = 0$$

$$8x + 28 + 15x - 25 + 66 = 0$$

$$23x + 69 = 0$$

$$23x = -69$$

$$x = -3$$

60. **(B)**

$$(2 + 3i)^3 = [(2 + 3i)(2 + 3i)](2 + 3i) = [4 + 6i + 6i + 9i^2](2 + 3i)$$

$$= [4 + 12i - 9](2 + 3i)$$

$$= [-5 + 12i](2 + 3i)$$

$$= -10 - 15i + 24i + 36i^2$$

$$= -10 + 9i - 36$$

$$= -46 + 9i$$

61. **(E)**

$$\sqrt{x^2 - 3x} = 2x - 6$$

$$(\sqrt{x^2 - 3x})^2 = (2x - 6)^2$$

$$x^2 - 3x = 4x^2 - 24x + 36$$
$$0 = 3x^2 - 21x + 36$$
$$0 = x^2 - 7x + 12$$
$$0 = (x - 3)(x - 4)$$
$$x - 3 = 0 \quad x - 4 = 0$$
$$x = 3 \qquad x = 4$$

Both checks work!

62. **(B)**

$$l_2: x + 3y - 6 = 0 \Rightarrow y = \frac{-1}{3}x + 2$$

Since the lines are perpendicular, we know that $m_1 \times m_2 = -1$. Therefore, $m_1 = 3$ $(3, 2)$

$$y - y_1 = m(x - x_1)$$
$$y - 2 = 3(x - 3)$$
$$y - 2 = 3x - 9$$
$$3x - y - 7 = 0$$

63. **(A)**

Center $= (0, 0)$

Radius $= 3$

$$(x - h)^2 + (y - k)^2 = r^2$$
$$(x - 0)^2 + (y - 0)^2 = (3)^2$$
$$x^2 + y^2 = 9$$

64. **(10)**

(All students) = (German speakers) + (Chinese speakers)

$\quad$ – (Speakers of both languages)

$$20 = 13 + 17 - x$$

Hence, $x = 10$.

65. **(D)**

$$A = \frac{h}{2}(b + B)$$

$$2(A) = 2\left[\frac{h}{2}(b + B)\right]$$

$$2A = h(b + B)$$

$$\frac{2A}{(b + B)} = \frac{h(b + B)}{(b + B)}$$

$$\frac{2A}{b + B} = h$$

66. **(B)** Roots are $x = 2 + \sqrt{3}$ and $x = 2 - \sqrt{3}$

$$x - 2 - \sqrt{3} = 0 \quad x - 2 + \sqrt{3} = 0$$

$$(x - 2 - \sqrt{3})(x - 2 + \sqrt{3}) = 0$$

$$x(x - 2 + \sqrt{3}) - 2(x - 2 + \sqrt{3}) - \sqrt{3}(x - 2 + \sqrt{3}) = 0$$

$$x^2 - 2x + x\sqrt{3} - 2x + 4 - 2\sqrt{3} - x\sqrt{3} + 2\sqrt{3} - 3 = 0$$

$$x^2 - 4x + 1 = 0$$

67. **(D)**

$$(a + bi) + (2 - 3i) = 2(-2 - 3i)$$

$$a + bi = 2(-2 + i) - (2 - 3i)$$

$$a + bi = -4 + 2i - 2 + 3i$$

$$a + bi = -6 + 5i$$

$$a = -6 \text{ and } b = 5$$

68. **(A)**

$$3x - 4y = 12 \Rightarrow y = \frac{3}{4}x - 3$$

$$Ax + 6y = -9 \Rightarrow y = \frac{-A}{6}x - \frac{3}{2}$$

Since the lines are parallel, we know that the slopes are equal.

$$\frac{3}{4} = \frac{-A}{6} \Rightarrow 12\left(\frac{3}{4}\right) = 12\left(\frac{-A}{6}\right)$$

$$9 = -2A \Rightarrow \frac{-9}{2} = A$$

69. **(E)**

$$3x^2 - 4x - 2$$

$$3\left(\frac{2-\sqrt{10}}{3}\right)^2 - 4\left(\frac{2-\sqrt{10}}{3}\right) - 2 = \frac{3(14-4\sqrt{10})}{9} - \frac{4(2-\sqrt{10})}{3} - 2$$

$$= \frac{14-4\sqrt{10}}{3} - \frac{8-4\sqrt{10}}{3} - \frac{6}{3}$$

$$= \frac{14-4\sqrt{10}-8+4\sqrt{10}-6}{3}$$

$$= \frac{14-8-6}{3} = \frac{14-14}{3} = \frac{0}{3} = 0$$

70. **(D)**

Tangent Line $\Rightarrow y = mx + b = 2x + b$

$$y = x^2 - 6x + 9$$

$$2x + b = x^2 - 6x + 9$$

$$0 = x^2 - 8x + (9 - b)$$

Since we want this equation to have only one solution, we know that

$$b^2 - 4ac = 0$$

$$(-8)^2 - 4(9 - b) = 0$$

$$64 - 36 + 4b = 0$$

$$4b = -28$$

$$b = -7$$

Therefore, $y = 2x - 7$

PRACTICE
TEST 3

CLEP COLLEGE ALGEBRA
Practice Test 3

(Answer sheets appear in the back of this book.)

TIME: 90 Minutes
         70 Questions

DIRECTIONS: Solve each problem, using any available space on the page for scratch work. Then either enter the correct numerical answer in the box provided, or decide which answer choice is the best and fill in the corresponding oval on the answer sheet.

NOTES:

(1) Unless otherwise specified, the domain of any function f is assumed to be the set of all real numbers x for which $f(x)$ is a real number.

(2) i will be used to denote $\sqrt{-1}$.

(3) All figures lie in a plane and are drawn to scale unless otherwise indicated.

1. Simplify $3a - 2 \{3a - 2[1 - 4(a - 1)] + 5\}$

   (A) $-4a + 10$

   (B) $-19a + 10$

   (C) $11a - 5$

   (D) $-22a + 10$

   (E) $9a^2 - 16a + 14$

2. Simplify the quotient $\dfrac{2x^0}{(2x)^0}$.

3. Multiply $(4x - 5)(6x - 7)$.

   (A) x^2

   (B) $24x^2 - 58x + 35$

   (C) $-34x + 35$

   (D) $-34x^2 + 35$

   (E) $24x^2 + 58x + 35$

4. Simplify $\dfrac{4x^3 + 6x^2}{2x}$.

   (A) $2x^2 + 3$

   (B) $8x^2$

   (C) $2x + 3$

   (D) $2x^3 + 3x^2$

   (E) $2x^2 + 3x$

5. In a school of 300 students, 260 students take physics and 185 students take calculus. How many students take both physics and calculus if we know that all the students take at least one of the courses?

6. Factor $x^2 + 7x + 12$.

   (A) $(x + 2)(x + 5)$

   (B) $(x + 2)(x + 6)$

   (C) $(x - 4)(x + 3)$

   (D) $(x + 4)(x + 3)$

   (E) Cannot be factored.

7. Simplify $\dfrac{x^2 - 3x}{x^2 - 9} + \dfrac{3}{x + 3}$.

   (A) $x + 3$

   (B) $x - 3$

   (C) $\dfrac{1}{3}$

   (D) $x^2 - 3x + 3$

   (E) 1

8. Combine

   $$\dfrac{3x + y}{x^2 - y^2} - \dfrac{2y}{x(x - y)} - \dfrac{1}{x + y}$$

   into a single fraction.

   (A) $\dfrac{2}{x}$

   (B) $\dfrac{2x^2 - 2xy + 2y^2}{x(x - y)(x + y)}$

   (C) $\dfrac{y}{2}$

   (D) $2x^2 - 2y^2$

   (E) $-2y$

9. Add the expressions

$4a^2 - 3 + 5a,$
$6a - 2a^2 + 2,$ and
$2a^2 - 3a + 8.$

(A) $12a + 7$

(D) $8a^2 - 12a + 13$

(B) $12a^2 - 8a + 15$

(E) 19

(C) $4a^2 + 8a + 7$

10. A chemist has 24 ounces of a 25% solution of argyrol. How much water must he add to reduce the strength of the argyrol to 20%?

11. Evaluate $\dfrac{12x^7 y}{3x^2 y^3}$.

(A) $\dfrac{9x^5}{y^2}$

(D) $\dfrac{4y^2}{x^5}$

(B) $\dfrac{4x^5}{y^2}$

(E) $4x^5 y^2$

(C) $4x^9 y^4$

12. Simplify the quotient

$$\frac{\sqrt{x}}{\sqrt[4]{x}}.$$

Write the result in exponential notation.

(A) x^2

(D) $x^{3/4}$

(B) $x^{1/4}$

(E) $x^{1/2}$

(C) x^{-2}

13. Simplify $\dfrac{x^2 - y^2}{x + y}$.

(A) xy

(D) $x - y$

(B) 0

(E) $x + y$

(C) $\dfrac{2(x - y)}{x + y}$

14. Simplify $\dfrac{1 + \dfrac{1}{x}}{1 - \dfrac{1}{x}}$.

(A) -1

(D) $\dfrac{x - 1}{x + 1}$

(B) $\dfrac{x^2 - 1}{x^2}$

(E) 0

(C) $\dfrac{x + 1}{x - 1}$

15. A haberdasher sold three shirts and four ties to one customer for $18.70. Another customer bought four shirts and seven ties of the same quality for $27.75. What was the price per shirt and price per tie?

(A) $3.95 (shirt), $1.65 (tie)

(B) $3.98 (tie), $1.69 (shirt)

(C) $3.95 (tie), $1.65 (shirt)

(D) $3.98 (shirt), $1.69 (tie)

(E) $4.02 (shirt), $1.64 (tie)

16. Subtract

$3x^4y^3 + 5x^2y - 4xy + 5x - 3$ from $5x^4y^3 - 3x^2y + 7$

(A) $-2x^4y^3 + 8x^2y - 4xy + 5x - 10$

(B) $2x^4y^3 + 2x^2y - 4xy + 5x + 4$

(C) $-16x^6y^4 - 20x^2y + 10$

(D) $2x^4y^3 - 8x^2y + 4xy - 5x + 10$

(E) $-2x^4y^3 - 2x^2y - 4xy + 5x + 4$

17. Subtract $4y^2 - 5y + 2$ from $7y^2 - 6$.

(A) $-3y^2 - 5y + 8$ (D) $-3y^2 + y + 2$

(B) $-3y^2 - 5y - 4$ (E) $3y^2 + 5y - 8$

(C) $3y^2 - 5y - 4$

18. Find the product: $(2x^2 - 3xy + y^2)(2x - y)$.

(A) $4x^3 - 8x^2y + 5xy^2 - y^3$ (D) $-4x^3y + 6x^2y^2 - 4xy^3$

(B) $4x^3 + 4x^2y - xy^2 - y^3$ (E) $4x^3 - 3x^2y^2 - y^3$

(C) $-2x^4y + x^3y^2 + 2xy^2 - y^3$

19. According to Hooke's Law, the amount of stretching of a spring, S, varies directly as the force, F, applied on the spring. In a spring to which Hooke's Law applies, a force of 18.6 lb stretches the spring by 1.27 in. Find k, the proportionality constant.

(A) 14.65 lb/in   (D) 23.62 lb/in

(B) 19.87 lb/in   (E) 15.92 lb/in

(C) 17.33 lb/in

20. Simplify $(x + 2y)(x - 2y)(x^2 + 4y^2)$.

(A) $x^4 + 4x^3y + 5x^2y^2 + 16xy^3 + 4y^4$

(B) $x^4 - 16y^4$

(C) $x^4 + 8x^2y^2 + 16y^4$

(D) $x^2 - 16y^2$

(E) $-16x^4y^4$

21. Find the indicated root $\sqrt[3]{-125}$.

    (A) -5 (D) 5

    (B) -25 (E) Cannot be evaluated.

    (C) 25

22. Simplify $5\sqrt{12} + 3\sqrt{75}$.

    (A) $95\sqrt{3}$ (D) 95

    (B) $15\sqrt{3}$ (E) $25\sqrt{3}$

    (C) $8\sqrt{87}$

23. Evaluate $\dfrac{-16x^{16}y^6z^4}{-4x^4y^2z^7}$.

    (A) $4x^{12}y^4z^3$ (D) $\dfrac{4x^4y^3}{z^3}$

    (B) $4x^{20}y^8z^{11}$ (E) $\dfrac{-4x^{12}y^4}{z^3}$

    (C) $\dfrac{4x^{12}y^4}{z^3}$

24. Divide $\dfrac{y^2+y-20}{y-3} + \dfrac{y^2-16}{y^2+y-12}$.

    (A) $y-4$ (D) $y+4$

    (B) $\dfrac{y+5}{y+4}$ (E) $y+5$

    (C) $y-3$

25. Perform the indicated operation: $\dfrac{3a-9b}{x-5} \times \dfrac{xy-5y}{ax-3bx}$.

(A) 0

(D) $\dfrac{y}{x}$

(B) $\dfrac{3}{x}$

(E) $\dfrac{a-3b}{x-5}$

(C) $\dfrac{3y}{x}$

26. Simplify $\sqrt[3]{16} + \sqrt[3]{54} - \sqrt[3]{24}$.

(A) $4 + 5\sqrt{6}$

(D) $3\sqrt[3]{2}$

(B) $5\sqrt[3]{2} - 2\sqrt[3]{3}$

(E) $5\sqrt{2} - \sqrt{3}$

(C) $3\sqrt[3]{2}$

27. Factor $a^4 - b^4$.

(A) $(a+b)^2 (a-b)^2$

(D) $(a-b)^4$

(B) $a+b$

(E) $a-b$

(C) $(a^2 + b^2)(a+b)(a-b)$

28. Multiply $(2\sqrt{3} + 3\sqrt{2}) \times (3\sqrt{3} - 2\sqrt{2})$.

(A) $48 + 5\sqrt{6}$

(D) $-6 + 5\sqrt{6}$

(B) -6

(E) $6 + 5\sqrt{6}$

(C) 6

29. Factor the expression $16a^2 - 4(b-c)^2$.

(A) $4(2a - b + c)(2a + b - c)$

(B) $4(2a - b + c)(2a - b + c)$

(C) $4(2a - bc)(2a + bc)$

(D) $4(2a - b - c)(2a + b - c)$

(E) $(2a - b + c)(2a + b - c)$

30. Find the expansion of $(x + y)^6$.

   (A) $x^6 + 3x^4y^2 + 3x^2y^4 + y^6$

   (B) $x^6 + y^6$

   (C) $x^6 + 5x^5y + 10x^4y^2 + 10x^3y^3 + 5x^2y + y^6$

   (D) $x^6 + 6x^5y + 15x^4y^2 + 20x^3y^3 + 15x^2y^4 + 6xy^5 + y^6$

   (E) $x^6 - 6x^5y - 15x^4y^2 - 20x^3y^3 - 15x^2y^4 - 6xy^5 - y^6$

31. Solve $9x - 5 = 7x + 3$.

   ┌─────────────┐
   │   │
   └─────────────┘

32. Solve the equation $\dfrac{1}{2}x + \dfrac{2}{3} = \dfrac{1}{4}x - \dfrac{1}{6}$.

   (A) 2   (D) $\dfrac{-5}{14}$

   (B) $\dfrac{-10}{3}$ (E) 3

   (C) -3

33. Solve the proportion $\dfrac{x+1}{4} = \dfrac{15}{22}$.

   (A) 4   (D) 3

   (B) 5   (E) 6

   (C) $\dfrac{7}{5}$

34. Solve $\sqrt{2}\,x - 2 = 2x - \sqrt{2}$.

   (A) 1   (D) -2

   (B) 2   (E) -1

   (C) 0

35. Solve the following for x: $6x^2 + 5x - 4 = 0$.

    (A) $\dfrac{-1}{6}$ and 0   (D) $\dfrac{-4}{3}$ and $\dfrac{1}{2}$

    (B) $\dfrac{-1}{2}$ and $\dfrac{4}{3}$ (E) -2 and $\dfrac{1}{3}$

    (C) $\dfrac{-1}{3}$ and 2

36. Solve the equation $2x^2 + 5x + 8 = 0$.

    (A) $\left(\dfrac{-5 + \sqrt{39}}{4}, \dfrac{-5 - \sqrt{39}}{4} \right)$

    (B) $\left(\dfrac{-1}{2}, -2 \right)$

    (C) $\left(\dfrac{-5 + i\sqrt{39}}{4}, \dfrac{-5 - i\sqrt{39}}{4} \right)$

    (D) $(-1, -4)$

    (E) No solution possible.

37. Solve $-3(x - 5) > x + 7$.

    (A) $x > 2$ (D) $x > 4$

    (B) $x < 4$ (E) $x < 2$

    (C) $x > \dfrac{11}{2}$

38. Find the solution set of the inequality $5x - 9 > 2x + 3$.

    (A) $x > 4$ (D) $x < 0$

    (B) $x > \dfrac{-6}{7}$ (E) $x > 3$

    (C) $x > 1$

39. Solve $10x - 7 \leq 6x + 5$.

   (A) $x \leq \dfrac{-1}{8}$ (D) $-x \leq \dfrac{3}{4}$

   (B) $x \geq 3$ (E) $x \leq 3$

   (C) $x \geq -3$

40. When an airplane flies at a speed of 300 miles per hour against the wind, it flies 200 miles in two hours. The windspeed is

   (A) 200 mph.   (D) 250 mph.

   (B) 150 mph.   (E) None of the above.

   (C) 100 mph.

41. Find the solution of the equation $\dfrac{4x - 7}{x - 2} = 3 + \dfrac{1}{x - 2}$.

   (A) 2   (D) $\dfrac{11}{4}$

   (B) $\dfrac{5}{6}$ (E) No solution possible.

   (C) 6

42. Solve $(x + 7)(x + 1) = x(x - 1) - 11$.

   (A) -6 (D) 2

   (B) $\dfrac{5}{3}$ (E) $\dfrac{-3}{7}$

   (C) -2

43. Find the equation for the line passing through $(3, 5)$ and $(-1, 2)$.

   (A) $2x - 4y = -5$ (D) $3x - 4y = -11$

   (B) $3x + 4y = 11$ (E) $3x - 5y = -13$

   (C) $x + 2y = 13$

44. Solve for x and y.

   $x + 2y = 8$

   $3x + 4y = 20$

   (A) $x = 0, y = 5$ (D) $x = 0, y = 4$

   (B) $x = 4, y = 2$ (E) $x = 2, y = 3$

   (C) $x = 8, y = 0$

45. Solve the system:

   $xy = 24$

   $y - 2x + 2 = 0$

   (A) $\{(-3, -8), (4, 6)\}$ (D) $\{(-3, 4), (-8, 6)\}$

   (B) $\{(-3, 6), (4, -8)\}$ (E) $\{(4, -3)\}$

   (C) $\{(-3, 4)\}$

46. A man buys a book for $20 and wishes to sell it. What price should he mark on it if he wishes a 40% discount while making a 50% profit on the cost price?

   (A) $25   (D) $50

   (B) $30   (E) $55

   (C) $40

47. Solve the following system:

   $x^2 + y^2 = 25$

   $2x + y = 10$

   (A) $\{(-3, 16), (-5, 20)\}$ (D) $\{(5, 0), (3, 4)\}$

   (B) $\{(0, 4)\}$ (E) $\{(4, 0)\}$

   (C) $\{(0, 5), (4, 3)\}$

48. Solve the equation $a^2x + 4c^2x - 10c = 5a - 4acx$, for x.

(A) $\dfrac{15}{a + 4ac + 4c}$

(D) $\dfrac{5}{a + 2c}$

(B) $\dfrac{5}{4ac}$

(E) $\dfrac{15ac}{(a + 2c)^2}$

(C) $\dfrac{15}{(a + 2c)^2}$

49. Find the solution of the equation $x^3 - 1 = 0$.

(A) $1, \dfrac{-1 - i\sqrt{3}}{2}$, and $\dfrac{-1 - i\sqrt{3}}{2}$

(B) 1 and -1

(C) $\dfrac{1}{2}$ and $\dfrac{-3}{2}$

(D) 1

(E) $1, \dfrac{1}{2}$, and $\dfrac{-3}{2}$

50. Solve the equation $x^3 - 16x = 0$.

(A) -4 and 4 (D) 16

(B) -2, 0, and 2 (E) 4

(C) -4, 0, and 4

51. Find the set $S = \{x \mid x^2 + 2x - 8 < 0\}$.

(A) $-4 < x < 2$ (D) $-2 < x < 4$

(B) $x < -2$ and $x > 4$ (E) $x > 2$ and $x < -4$

(C) $-2 < x < 2$

52. Obtain the solution set of $2x^2 > x + 6$.

(A) $x < -2$ and $x > \dfrac{3}{2}$

(D) $x > 1$ and $x < \dfrac{-3}{2}$

(B) $\dfrac{-3}{2} < x < 1$

(E) $x > 2$ and $x < \dfrac{-3}{2}$

(C) $\dfrac{-3}{2} < x < 2$

53. If the cost of five apples is $3.25, and if the cost of an orange and one of these apples together is $1.05, what is the cost of an orange alone?

(A) $0.35

(D) $0.50

(B) $0.40

(E) $0.55

(C) $0.45

54. Evaluate

$$p = \dfrac{(a-b)(ab+c)}{(cb-2a)}$$

when $a = 2$, $b = -\frac{1}{2}$, and $c = -3$.

(A) 4

(D) $2\dfrac{2}{5}$

(B) -2

(E) -4

(C) $\dfrac{2}{5}$

55. If $g(x) = x^2 + 5x - 3$, find $g(-7)$.

(A) -11

(D) 11

(B) -87

(E) 17

(C) -17

56. Express $\left(\dfrac{a^{-2}}{b^{-3}}\right)^2$ using only positive exponents.

(A) $\dfrac{a}{b^3}$ (D) $\dfrac{b^6}{a^4}$

(B) $\dfrac{a^4}{b^6}$ (E) a^2b^3

(C) ab^3

57. Simplify the quotient $\dfrac{(x^{-2}y^4)^3}{(xy)^{-3}}$.

(A) $\dfrac{y^{15}}{x^3}$ (D) $-x^3y^9$

(B) x^3y^9 (E) $\dfrac{x^3}{y^{15}}$

(C) $\dfrac{y^9}{x^3}$

58. Simplify the expression $xy(x^{-1} + y^{-1})$.

(A) $y + x$ (D) $-x^2y - xy^2$

(B) $\dfrac{1}{y} + \dfrac{1}{x}$ (E) $\dfrac{xy}{x + y}$

(C) $y - x$

59. John is four times as old as Harry. In six years John will be twice as old as Harry. How old is Harry now?

60. Find the roots of the function G defined by the rule $G(x) = x^2 + 5x + 6$.

    (A) 1, 5, and 6
    (B) −2 and −3
    (C) 1

    (D) −1 and −6
    (E) 2 and 3

TEST STOPS HERE. *EXTRA PRACTICE FOLLOWS...*

61. Find $\log_9\left(\dfrac{1}{27}\right)$.

    (A) $\dfrac{-3}{2}$
    (B) 2
    (C) $\dfrac{3}{2}$

    (D) −3
    (E) $\dfrac{2}{3}$

62. Find the value of x if $\log_4 64 = x$.

63. Solve the equation $2^{3x} = 4^{x+1}$.

    (A) 2
    (B) 1
    (C) 3

    (D) $\dfrac{1}{2}$
    (E) 4

64. If $\log_3 N = 2$, find N.

    (A) $\dfrac{3}{2}$
    (B) 9
    (C) 6

    (D) $\log_2 3$
    (E) $\dfrac{2}{3}$

65. If the cost of a dozen pencils and a dozen pens together is $16.20, and if the cost of a pencil is $0.15, what is the cost of a pen?

(A) $1.20
(D) $1.55

(B) $1.35
(E) $1.60

(C) $1.40

66. If $f(t) = 6t + 13$, find $f(5) - f(4)$.

67. If $f(x) = x^2 - x - 3$,

$$g(x) = \frac{x^2 - 1}{x + 2},$$

and $h(x) = f(x) + g(x)$, find $h(2)$.

(A) $\dfrac{-1}{4}$
(D) -2

(B) -1
(E) $\dfrac{7}{4}$

(C) $\dfrac{-3}{2}$

68. If $\log_b 2 = 0.69$ and $\log_b 3 = 1.10$, find $\log_b 6$.

(A) 0.759
(D) 2.07

(B) 1.79
(E) 0.41

(C) 2.20

69. Determine the range of the following function:

$$f(x) = |x - 7|.$$

(A) $y \geq 7$
(D) $y \leq -7$

(B) $y \leq 7$
(E) $x \leq 0$

(C) $y \geq 0$

70. Let f be the function whose domain is the set of all real numbers, whose range is the set of all numbers greater than or equal to 2, and whose rule of correspondence is given by the equation

$f(x) = x^2 + 2.$

Find $3f(0) + f(-1)\,f(2)$.

CLEP COLLEGE ALGEBRA
TEST 3

ANSWER KEY

1.	(B)	19.	(A)	37.	(E)	55.	(D)
2.	(2)	20.	(B)	38.	(A)	56.	(B)
3.	(B)	21.	(A)	39.	(E)	57.	(A)
4.	(E)	22.	(E)	40.	(A)	58.	(A)
5.	(145)	23.	(C)	41.	(A)	59.	(3)
6.	(D)	24.	(E)	42.	(C)	60.	(B)
7.	(E)	25.	(C)	43.	(D)	61.	(A)
8.	(A)	26.	(B)	44.	(B)	62.	(3)
9.	(C)	27.	(C)	45.	(A)	63.	(A)
10.	(6)	28.	(E)	46.	(D)	64.	(B)
11.	(B)	29.	(A)	47.	(D)	65.	(A)
12.	(B)	30.	(D)	48.	(D)	66.	(6)
13.	(D)	31.	(4)	49.	(A)	67.	(A)
14.	(C)	32.	(B)	50.	(C)	68.	(B)
15.	(D)	33.	(A)	51.	(A)	69.	(C)
16.	(D)	34.	(E)	52.	(E)	70.	(24)
17.	(E)	35.	(D)	53.	(B)		
18.	(A)	36.	(C)	54.	(A)		

DETAILED EXPLANATIONS
OF ANSWERS

TEST 3

1. **(B)**

$$3a - 2\{3a - 2[1 - 4(a-1)] + 5\} = 3a - 2\{3a - 2[1 - 4a + 4] + 5\}$$
$$= 3a - 2\{3a - 2[5 - 4a] + 5\}$$
$$= 3a - 2\{3a - 10 + 8a + 5\}$$
$$= 3a - 2\{11a - 5\}$$
$$= 3a - 22a + 10$$
$$= -19a + 10$$

2. **(2)**

$$\frac{2x^0}{(2x)^0} = \frac{2(1)}{1} = \frac{2}{1} = 2$$

3. **(B)**

$$(4x - 5)(6x - 7) = (4x)(6x) + (4x)(-7) + (-5)(6x) + (-5)(-7)$$
$$= 24x^2 - 28x - 30x + 35$$
$$= 24x^2 - 58x + 35$$

4. **(E)**

$$\frac{4x^3 + 6x^2}{2x} = \frac{2x^2(2x + 3)}{2x}$$
$$= x(2x + 3)$$
$$= 2x^2 + 3x$$

5. **(145)**

[all students] = [students taking physics]

+ [students taking calculus] − [those taking both]

This formula is a direct conclusion of the following relation:

$$n(A \cup B) = n(A) + n(B) - n(A \cap B)$$

while A and B are two sets and n stands for the number of elements a set has. In the above formula, if we define A as the set of students who are taking physics and B as the set of students taking calculus, then $n(A) = 260$ and $n(B) = 185$ and we have $n(A \cup B) = 300$, because each student at least takes one of the two courses. Therefore, $(A \cap B)$ will be the set of students taking both of the courses and $n(A \cap B)$ can be derived from the above relation. The following diagram shows the validity of the equation.

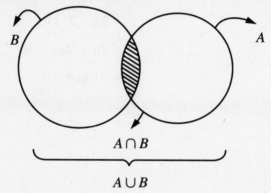

$A \cap B$

$A \cup B$

The students taking both courses are counted twice in $[n(A) + n(B)]$ and therefore must be subtracted from the sum of students taking individual courses.

We obtain

$$300 = 260 + 185 - x$$

$$= 445 - x$$

Hence, $x = 145.$

6. **(D)**

$$x^2 + 7x + 12$$

$A = 1$ $B = 7$ $C = 12$

$AC = 12$ $B = 7$

$$x^2 + 4x + 3x + 12 = x(x + 4) + 3(x + 4)$$

$$= (x + 4)(x + 3)$$

7. **(E)**

$$\frac{x^2 - 3x}{x^2 - 9} + \frac{3}{x + 3} = \frac{x(x - 3)}{(x + 3)(x - 3)} + \frac{3}{x + 3}$$

$$= \frac{x}{x + 3} + \frac{3}{x + 3}$$

$$= \frac{x + 3}{(x + 3)} = 1$$

8. **(A)**

$$\frac{3x + y}{x^2 - y^2} - \frac{2y}{x(x - y)} - \frac{1}{x + y}$$

$$= \frac{x(3x + y)}{x(x - y)(x + y)} - \frac{2y(x + y)}{x(x - y)(x + y)} - \frac{x(x - y)(1)}{x(x - y)(x + y)}$$

$$= \frac{3x^2 + xy - 2xy - 2y^2 - x^2 + xy}{x(x - y)(x + y)}$$

$$= \frac{2x^2 - 2y^2}{x(x - y)(x + y)} = \frac{2(x - y)(x + y)}{x(x - y)(x + y)} = \frac{2}{x}$$

9. **(C)**

$$(4a^2 - 3 + 5a) + (6a - 2a^2 + 2) + (2a^2 - 3a + 8)$$

$$= 4a^2 - 3 + 5a + 6a - 2a^2 + 2 + 2a^2 - 3a + 8$$

$$= 4a^2 + 8a + 7$$

10. **(6)**   Let x = number of ounces of water to be added. The relationship used to set up the equation is (since only water is added):

Amount of argyrol in new mixture

= Amount of argyrol in old mixture

$$.20(24 + x) = .25(24)$$
$$4.8 + .2x = 6$$
$$2x = 12$$
$$x = 6 \text{ ounces of water}$$

The new mixture has 30 ounces. Of this, 6 ounces (or 20%) is argyrol.

11. **(B)**

$$\frac{12x^7y}{3x^2y^3} = \frac{12}{3} \times \frac{x^7}{x^2} \times \frac{y^1}{y^3}$$

$$= -4x^{7-2}y^{1-3}$$

$$= 4x^5y^{-2}$$

$$= \frac{4x^5}{y^2}$$

12. **(B)**

$$\frac{\sqrt{x}}{\sqrt[4]{x}} = \frac{x^{1/2}}{x^{1/4}} = x^{1/2-1/4}$$

$$= x^{2/4-1/4}$$

$$= x^{1/4}$$

13. **(D)**

$$\frac{x^2 - y^2}{x+y} = \frac{(x+y)(x-y)}{(x+y)}$$

$$= x - y$$

14. **(C)**

$$\frac{1+\dfrac{1}{x}}{1-\dfrac{1}{x}} = \frac{\dfrac{x}{x}+\dfrac{1}{x}}{\dfrac{x}{x}-\dfrac{1}{x}}$$

$$= \frac{\dfrac{x+1}{x}}{\dfrac{x-1}{x}}$$

$$= \frac{x+1}{x} \times \frac{x}{x-1} = \frac{x+1}{x-1}$$

15. **(D)**

Let x = Cost of one shirt

y = Cost of one tie

$3x + 4y = 1,870$ (1)

$4x + 7y = 2,775$ (2)

When the equations are solved simultaneously, it is found that $x =$ 398, i.e., the price of a shirt is \$3.98 and $y = 169$, i.e., the price of a tie is \$1.69.

16. **(D)**

$$(5x^4y^3 - 3x^2y + 7) - (3x^4y^3 + 5x^2y - 4xy + 5x - 3)$$

$$= 5x^4y^3 - 3x^2y + 7 - 3x^4y^3 - 5x^2y + 4xy - 5x + 3$$

$$= 2x^4y^3 - 8x^2y + 4xy - 5x + 10$$

17. **(E)**

$$(7y^2 - 6) - (4y^2 - 5y + 2) = 7y^2 - 6 - 4y^2 + 5y - 2$$

$$= 3y^2 + 5y - 8$$

18. **(A)**

$$(2x^2 - 3xy + y^2)(2x - y) = 2x^2(2x - y) - 3xy(2x - y) + y^2(2x - y)$$

$$= 2x^2(2x) + 2x^2(-y) - 3xy(2x) - 3xy(-y) + y^2(2x) + y^2(-y)$$

$$= 4x^3 - 2x^2y - 6x^2y + 3xy^2 + 2xy^2 - y^3$$

$$= 4x^3 - 8x^2y + 5xy^2 - y^3$$

19. **(A)** The direct variation of the amount of stretching of the spring, S, and the force applied on it, F, is expressed symbolically as

$F = kS$, where k is the constant of proportionality.

We are given that $F = 18.6$ lb and $S = 1.27$ in. Thus, it is necessary merely to substitute the given values in the equation $F = kS$, obtaining

$$18.6 = k\,(1.27),$$

from which $k = 18.6/1.27 = 14.65$ lb/in.

20. **(B)**

$$[(x + 2y)\,(x - 2y)]\,(x^2 + 4y^2) = [x^2 - 4y^2]\,(x^2 + 4y^2)$$
$$= x^4 - 16y^4$$

21. **(A)**

$$\sqrt[3]{-125} = \sqrt[3]{(-5)^3}$$
$$= (\sqrt[3]{-5})^3 = -5$$

22. **(E)**

$$5\sqrt{12} + 3\sqrt{75} = 5\sqrt{4 \times 3} + 3\sqrt{25 \times 3}$$
$$= 5\sqrt{4}\sqrt{3} + 3\sqrt{25}\sqrt{3}$$
$$= 5(2)\sqrt{3} + 3(5)\sqrt{3}$$
$$= 10\sqrt{3} + 15\sqrt{3}$$
$$= 25\sqrt{3}$$

23. **(C)**

$$\frac{-16x^{16}y^6z^4}{-4x^4y^2z^7} = \frac{-16}{-4} \times \frac{x^{16}}{x^4} \times \frac{y^6}{y^2} \times \frac{z^4}{z^7}$$
$$= 4x^{16-4}y^{6-2}z^{4-7}$$
$$= 4x^{12}y^4z^{-3}$$
$$= \frac{4x^{12}y^4}{z^3}$$

24. **(E)**

$$\frac{y^2 + y - 20}{y - 3} + \frac{y^2 - 16}{y^2 + y - 12} = \frac{(y + 5)(y - 4)}{y - 3} + \frac{(y - 4)(y + 4)}{(y + 4)(y - 3)}$$

$$= \frac{(y+5)(y-4)}{(y-3)} \times \frac{(y+4)(y-3)}{(x-4)(y+4)}$$

$$= y+5$$

25. **(C)**

$$\frac{3a-9b}{x-5} \times \frac{xy-5y}{ax-3bx} = \frac{3(a-3b)}{x-5} \times \frac{y(x-5)}{x(a-3b)}$$

$$= \frac{3y}{x}$$

26. **(B)**

$$\sqrt[3]{16} + \sqrt[3]{54} - \sqrt[3]{24} = \sqrt[3]{8 \times 2} + \sqrt[3]{27 \times 2} + \sqrt[3]{8 \times 3}$$

$$= \sqrt[3]{8}\sqrt[3]{2} + \sqrt[3]{27}\sqrt[3]{2} - \sqrt[3]{8}\sqrt[3]{3}$$

$$= 2\sqrt[3]{2} + 3\sqrt[3]{2} - 2\sqrt[3]{3}$$

$$= 5\sqrt[3]{2} - 2\sqrt[3]{3}$$

27. **(C)**

$$a^4 - b^4 = (a^2 + b^2)(a^2 - b^2)$$

$$= (a^2 + b^2)(a+b)(a-b)$$

28. **(E)**

$$(2\sqrt{3} + 3\sqrt{2})(3\sqrt{3} - 2\sqrt{2})$$

$$= (2\sqrt{3})(3\sqrt{3}) + (2\sqrt{3})(-2\sqrt{2}) + (3\sqrt{2})(3\sqrt{3}) + (3\sqrt{2})(-2\sqrt{2})$$

$$= 6(3) - 4\sqrt{2}\sqrt{3} + 9\sqrt{2}\sqrt{3} - 6(2)$$

$$= 18 - 4\sqrt{2 \times 3} + 9\sqrt{2 \times 3} - 12$$

$$= 18 - 4\sqrt{6} + 9\sqrt{6} - 12$$

$$= 6 + 5\sqrt{6}$$

29. **(A)**

$$16a^2 - 4(b-c)^2$$

$$4[4a^2 - (b-c)^2]$$

$$4 [2a - (b - c)] [2a + (b - c)]$$
$$4 [2a - b + c] [2a + b - c]$$

30. **(D)**

$$
\begin{array}{ccccccccccccc}
 & & & & & & 1 & & & & & & \\
 & & & & & 1 & & 1 & & & & & \\
 & & & & 1 & & 2 & & 1 & & & & \\
 & & & 1 & & 3 & & 3 & & 1 & & & \\
 & & 1 & & 4 & & 6 & & 4 & & 1 & & \\
 & 1 & & 5 & & 10 & & 10 & & 5 & & 1 & \\
1 & & 6 & & 15 & & 20 & & 15 & & 6 & & 1 \\
\end{array}
$$

$$(x + y)^6 = x^6 + 6x^5y + 15x^4y^2 + 20x^3y^3 + 15x^2y^4 + 6xy^5 + y^6$$

31. **(4)**

$$9x - 5 = 7x + 3$$
$$2x - 5 = 3$$
$$2x = 8$$
$$x = 4$$

32. **(B)**

$$\frac{1}{2}x + \frac{2}{3} = \frac{1}{4}x - \frac{1}{6}$$

$$12\left(\frac{1}{2}x\right) + 12\left(\frac{2}{3}\right) = 12\left(\frac{1}{4}x\right) - 12\left(\frac{1}{6}\right)$$

$$6x + 8 = 3x - 2$$
$$3x + 8 = -2$$
$$3x = -10$$
$$x = \frac{-10}{3}$$

33. **(A)**

$$\frac{x+1}{4} = \frac{15}{12}$$

$$12(x+1) = 4 \times 15$$

$$12x + 12 = 60$$

$$12x = 48$$

$$x = 4$$

34. **(E)**

$$\sqrt{2}\,x - 2 = 2x - \sqrt{2}$$

$$\sqrt{2}\,x - 2x = 2 - \sqrt{2}$$

$$(\sqrt{2} - 2)x = 2 - \sqrt{2}$$

$$x = \frac{2 - \sqrt{2}}{\sqrt{2} - 2} = \frac{-1(\sqrt{2} - 2)}{\sqrt{2} - 2} = -1$$

35. **(D)**

$$6x^2 + 5x - 4 = 0$$

$$(3x + 4)(2x - 1) = 0$$

$$3x + 4 = 0 \qquad 2x - 1 = 0$$

$$3x = -4 \qquad 2x = 1$$

$$x = \frac{-4}{3} \qquad x = \frac{1}{2}$$

36. **(C)**

$$2x^2 + 5x + 8 = 0$$

$$x = \frac{-5 \pm \sqrt{5^2 - 4(2)(8)}}{2(2)}$$

$$x = \frac{-5 \pm \sqrt{25 - 64}}{4}$$

$$x = \frac{-5 \pm \sqrt{-39}}{4} = \frac{-5 \pm i\sqrt{39}}{4}$$

37. **(E)**

$$-3(x - 5) > x + 7$$

$$-3x + 15 > x + 7$$

$$-4x + 15 > 7$$

$$-4x > -8$$

$$x < 2$$

38. **(A)**

$$5x - 9 > 2x + 3$$

$$3x - 9 > 3$$

$$3x > 12$$

$$x > 4$$

39. **(E)**

$$10x - 7 \leq 6x + 5$$

$$4x - 7 \leq 5$$

$$4x \leq 12$$

$$x \leq 3$$

40. **(A)**   Let x = the speed of the wind.

$300 - x$ = the speed of the plane relative to the ground.

Since speed × time = distance, solve for x.

$$(300 - x)(2) = 200$$

$$600 - 2x = 200$$

$$2x = 400$$

$$x = 200 \text{ mph}$$

41. **(A)**

$$\frac{4x-7}{x-2} = 3 + \frac{1}{x-2}$$

$$(x-2)\left[\frac{4x-7}{x-2}\right] = (x-2)[3] + (x-2)\left[\frac{1}{x-2}\right]$$

$$4x - 7 = 3x - 6 + 1$$

$$4x - 7 = 3x - 5$$

$$x - 7 = -5$$

$$x = 2$$

But $x = 2$ will not work in the original equation. It would cause the denominator of two of the fractions to become zero. Therefore, there is no solution possible.

42. **(C)**

$$(x + 7)(x + 1) = x(x - 1) - 11$$

$$x^2 + 8x + 7 = x^2 - x - 11$$

$$8x + 7 = -x - 11$$

$$9x + 7 = -11$$

$$9x = -18$$

$$x = -2$$

43. **(D)**

$$(3, 5) \quad (-1, 2)$$

$$m = \frac{y_2 - y_1}{x_2 - x_1} = \frac{2 - 5}{-1 - 3} = \frac{3}{4}$$

$$y - y_1 = m(x - x_1)$$

$$y - 2 = \frac{3}{4}[x - (-1)]$$

$$4(y - 2) = 3[x + 1]$$

$$4y - 8 = 3x + 3$$

$$3x - 4y = -11$$

44. **(B)**

$$x + 2y = 8 \rightarrow x = -2y + 8$$
$$3x + 4y = 20$$
$$3(-2y + 8) + 4y = 20$$
$$-6y + 24 + 4y = 20$$
$$-2y + 24 = 20$$
$$-2y = -4$$
$$y = 2$$
$$x = -2y + 8$$
$$x = -2(2) + 8$$
$$= -4 + 8$$
$$x = 4$$

Therefore, $x = 4$ and $y = 2$.

45. **(A)**

$$y - 2x + 2 = 0 \rightarrow y = 2x - 2$$
$$xy = 24$$
$$x(2x - 2) = 2x^2 - 2x = 24$$
$$2x^2 - 2x - 24 = 0$$
$$x^2 - x - 12 = 0$$
$$(x + 3)(x - 4) = 0$$
$$x + 3 = 0$$
$$x = -3$$
$$x - 4 = 0$$
$$x = 4$$

$y = 2x - 2$	$y = 2x - 2$
$y = 2(-3) - 2$	$y = 2(4) - 2$
$y = -6 - 2$	$y = 8 - 2$
$y = -8$	$y = 6$

Therefore, $\{(-3, -8), (4, 6)\}$.

46. **(D)** The man originally buys the book for $20. He wishes to make a 50% profit on the book. To do this he must sell the book for:

$$20 + (50\%)(20) = \$30.$$

He would like the $30 price to appear as if it is a mark down from an even higher price. We must find this phony price. Let this price be p. Then:

$$p - (40\%)(p) = 30$$

$$(.60)p = 30$$

$$p = \$50$$

47. **(D)**

$$2x + y = 10 \rightarrow y = 10 - 2x$$

$$x^2 + y^2 = 25$$

$$x^2 + (10 - 2x)^2 = 25$$

$$x^2 + 100 - 40x + 4x^2 = 25$$

$$5x^2 - 40x + 100 = 25$$

$$5x^2 - 40x + 75 = 0$$

$$x^2 - 8x + 15 = 0$$

$$(x - 5)(x - 3) = 0$$

$$x - 5 = 0 \qquad x - 3 = 0$$

$$x = 5 \qquad x = 3$$

$$y = 10 - 2x \qquad y = 10 - 2x$$

$$y = 10 - 2(5) \qquad y = 10 - 2(3)$$

$$y = 0 \qquad y = 4$$

Therefore, $(5, 0)$ and $(3, 4)$ are solutions.

48. **(D)**

$$a^2x + 4c^2x - 10c = 5a - 4acx$$

$$a^2x + 4acx + 4c^2x = 5a + 10c$$

$$(a^2 + 4ac + 4c^2)x = 5(a + 2c)$$

$$(a + 2c)^2 x = 5(a + 2c)$$

$$x = \frac{5(a + 2c)}{(a + 2c)^2}$$

$$x = \frac{5}{a + 2c}$$

49. **(A)**

$$x^3 - 1 = 0$$

$$(x - 1)(x^2 + x + 1) = 0$$

$$x - 1 = 0 \qquad\qquad x^2 + x + 1 = 0$$

$$x = 1$$

$$x = \frac{-1 \pm \sqrt{(1)^2 - 4(1)(1)}}{2(1)}$$

$$x = \frac{-1 \pm \sqrt{1 - 4}}{2} = \frac{-1 \pm \sqrt{-3}}{2} = \frac{-1 \pm i\sqrt{3}}{2}$$

$\therefore$ the solutions are 1, $\dfrac{-1 + i\sqrt{3}}{2}$, and $\dfrac{-1 - i\sqrt{3}}{2}$

50. **(C)**

$$x^3 - 16x = 0$$

$$x(x^2 - 16) = 0$$

$$x(x - 4)(x + 4) = 0$$

$$x = 0 \qquad\qquad x - 4 = 0 \qquad\qquad x + 4 = 0$$

$$x = 0 \qquad\qquad x = 4 \qquad\qquad x = -4$$

Therefore, the solutions are −4, 0, and 4.

51. **(A)**

$$x^2 + 2x - 8 < 0$$

$$(x + 4)(x - 2) < 0$$

$$x + 4 = 0 \qquad\qquad x - 2 = 0$$

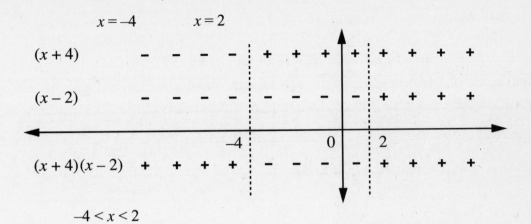

$$-4 < x < 2$$

52. **(E)**

$$2x^2 > x + 6$$

$$2x^2 - x - 6 > 0$$

$$(2x + 3)(x - 2) > 0$$

$$2x + 3 = 0 \qquad x - 2 = 0$$

$$x = \frac{-3}{2} \qquad x = 2$$

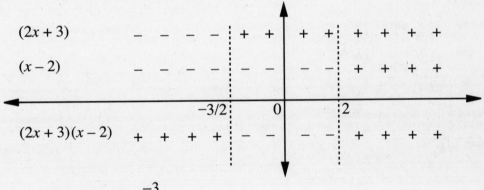

$$x > 2 \text{ and } x < \frac{-3}{2}$$

53. **(B)**

$$\text{Cost of an apple} = \frac{\$3.25}{5}$$

$$= \$0.65$$

$$\text{Cost of an orange} = \$1.05 - \$0.65$$

$$= \$0.40$$

54. **(A)**

$$p = \frac{(a-b)(ab+c)}{(cb-2a)} = \frac{[2-(-\frac{1}{2})][2(-\frac{1}{2})+(-3)]}{[(-3)(-\frac{1}{2})-2(2)]}$$

$$p = \frac{[2+\frac{1}{2}][-1-3]}{\frac{3}{2}-4} = \frac{[\frac{4}{2}+\frac{1}{2}][-4]}{\frac{3}{2}-\frac{8}{2}}$$

$$p = \frac{[\frac{5}{2}][\frac{-4}{1}]}{\frac{-5}{2}} = \frac{\frac{-10}{1}}{\frac{-5}{2}} = \frac{-10}{1} = \frac{-2}{5}$$

$$p = 4$$

55. **(D)**

$$g(x) = x^2 + 5x - 3$$

$$g(-7) = (-7)^2 + 5\,(-7) - 3$$

$$g(-7) = 49 - 35 - 3$$

$$g(-7) = 11$$

56. **(B)**

$$\left(\frac{a^{-2}}{b^{-3}}\right)^{-2} = \frac{(a^{-2})^{-2}}{(b^{-3})^{-2}}$$

$$= \frac{a^{(-2)\times(-2)}}{b^{(-3)\times(-2)}} = \frac{a^4}{b^6}$$

57. **(A)**

$$\frac{(x^{-2}y^4)^3}{(xy)^{-3}} = \frac{(x^{-2})^3(y^4)^3}{(x)^{-3}(y)^{-3}}$$

$$= \frac{x^{(-2)\times(3)}y^{(4)\times(3)}}{x^{-3}y^{-3}}$$

$$= \frac{x^{-6}y^{12}}{x^{-3}y^{-3}}$$

$$= x^{-6-(-3)}y^{12-(-3)}$$

$$= x^{-6+3}y^{12+3}$$

$$= x^{-3}y^{15} = \frac{y^{15}}{x^3}$$

58. **(A)**

$$xy(x^{-1} + y^{-1}) = xy\left(\frac{1}{x} + \frac{1}{y}\right)$$

$$= \frac{xy}{x} + \frac{xy}{y}$$

$$= y + x$$

59. **(3)**

	Now	In six years
John's age	$4x$	$4x + 6$
Harry's age	x	$x + 6$

$4x + 6 = 2(x + 6)$

$4 + 6 = 2x + 12$

$2x = 6$

$x = 3$

Therefore, Harry is now three years old.

60. **(B)**

$$G(x) = x^2 + 5x + 6$$

$$x^2 + 5x + 6 = 0$$

$$(x + 3)(x + 2) = 0$$

$x + 3 = 0 \qquad x + 2 = 0$

$x = -3 \qquad\quad x = -2$

61. **(A)**

$$\log_9\left(\frac{1}{27}\right) = E$$

$$(9)^E = \frac{1}{27}$$

$$(3^2)^E = \frac{1}{3^3}$$

$$3^{2E} = 3^{-3}$$

$$2E = -3$$

$$E = \frac{-3}{2}$$

62. **(3)**

$$\log_4 64 = x$$

$$4^x = 64$$

$$4^x = 4^3$$

$$x = 3$$

63. **(A)**

$$2^{3x} = 4^{x+1}$$

$$2^{3x} = (2^2)^{x+1}$$

$$2^{3x} = 2^{2(x+1)}$$

$$3x = 2(x+1)$$

$$3x = 2x + 2$$

$$x = 2$$

64. **(B)**

$$\log_3 N = 2$$

$$3^2 = N$$

$$9 = N$$

65. **(A)** Cost of one pen and one pencil equals

$$\frac{\$16.20}{12} = \$1.35.$$

Cost of one pen equals

$$\$1.35 - \$0.15 = \$1.20.$$

66. **(6)**

$$f(5) - f(4) = [6(5) + 13] - [6(4) + 13]$$
$$= [30 + 13] - [24 + 13]$$
$$= 43 - 37$$
$$= 6$$

67. **(A)**

$$h(x) = [f(x)] + [g(x)]$$

$$h(x) = [x^2 - x - 3] + \left[\frac{x^2 - 1}{x + 2}\right]$$

$$h(2) = [(2)^2 - (2) - 3] + \left[\frac{(2)^2 - 1}{2 + 2}\right]$$

$$h(2) = [4 - 2 - 3] + \left[\frac{4 - 1}{4}\right]$$

$$h(2) = [-1] + \left[\frac{3}{4}\right] = \frac{-4}{4} + \frac{3}{4}$$

$$h(2) = \frac{-1}{4}$$

68. **(B)**

$$\log_b 6 = \log_b (2 \times 3)$$
$$= \log_b 2 + \log_b 3$$
$$= 0.69 + 1.10$$
$$= 1.79$$

69. **(C)**

$$f(x) = |x - 7|$$

The absolute value function gives us the "distance between 7 and a number represented by x." Since we measure distances with positive numbers, we know that the range of this function must be greater than or equal to zero.

Range: $y \geq 0$

70. **(24)**

$$f(x) = x^2 + 2$$
$$= 3[f(0)] + [f(-1)] \, [f(2)]$$
$$= 3[(0)^2 + 2] + [(-1)^2 + 2] \, [(2)^2 + 2]$$
$$= 3[0 + 2] + [1 + 2] \, [4 + 2]$$
$$= 3[2] + [3] \, [6] = 6 + 18 = 24$$

ANSWER SHEETS

CLEP COLLEGE ALGEBRA
TEST 1

1. Ⓐ Ⓑ Ⓒ Ⓓ Ⓔ
2. Ⓐ Ⓑ Ⓒ Ⓓ Ⓔ
3. Ⓐ Ⓑ Ⓒ Ⓓ Ⓔ
4. Ⓐ Ⓑ Ⓒ Ⓓ Ⓔ
5. Ⓐ Ⓑ Ⓒ Ⓓ Ⓔ
6. Ⓐ Ⓑ Ⓒ Ⓓ Ⓔ
7. Ⓐ Ⓑ Ⓒ Ⓓ Ⓔ
8. Ⓐ Ⓑ Ⓒ Ⓓ Ⓔ
9. Ⓐ Ⓑ Ⓒ Ⓓ Ⓔ
10. Ⓐ Ⓑ Ⓒ Ⓓ Ⓔ
11. Ⓐ Ⓑ Ⓒ Ⓓ Ⓔ
12. Ⓐ Ⓑ Ⓒ Ⓓ Ⓔ
13. Ⓐ Ⓑ Ⓒ Ⓓ Ⓔ
14. [   ]
15. Ⓐ Ⓑ Ⓒ Ⓓ Ⓔ
16. Ⓐ Ⓑ Ⓒ Ⓓ Ⓔ
17. Ⓐ Ⓑ Ⓒ Ⓓ Ⓔ
18. Ⓐ Ⓑ Ⓒ Ⓓ Ⓔ
19. [   ]
20. Ⓐ Ⓑ Ⓒ Ⓓ Ⓔ
21. Ⓐ Ⓑ Ⓒ Ⓓ Ⓔ
22. Ⓐ Ⓑ Ⓒ Ⓓ Ⓔ
23. Ⓐ Ⓑ Ⓒ Ⓓ Ⓔ
24. Ⓐ Ⓑ Ⓒ Ⓓ Ⓔ
25. [   ]
26. Ⓐ Ⓑ Ⓒ Ⓓ Ⓔ
27. Ⓐ Ⓑ Ⓒ Ⓓ Ⓔ
28. Ⓐ Ⓑ Ⓒ Ⓓ Ⓔ
29. Ⓐ Ⓑ Ⓒ Ⓓ Ⓔ
30. Ⓐ Ⓑ Ⓒ Ⓓ Ⓔ
31. Ⓐ Ⓑ Ⓒ Ⓓ Ⓔ
32. Ⓐ Ⓑ Ⓒ Ⓓ Ⓔ
33. Ⓐ Ⓑ Ⓒ Ⓓ Ⓔ
34. Ⓐ Ⓑ Ⓒ Ⓓ Ⓔ
35. Ⓐ Ⓑ Ⓒ Ⓓ Ⓔ

36. Ⓐ Ⓑ Ⓒ Ⓓ Ⓔ
37. Ⓐ Ⓑ Ⓒ Ⓓ Ⓔ
38. [   ]
39. [   ]
40. Ⓐ Ⓑ Ⓒ Ⓓ Ⓔ
41. Ⓐ Ⓑ Ⓒ Ⓓ Ⓔ
42. Ⓐ Ⓑ Ⓒ Ⓓ Ⓔ
43. Ⓐ Ⓑ Ⓒ Ⓓ Ⓔ
44. Ⓐ Ⓑ Ⓒ Ⓓ Ⓔ
45. Ⓐ Ⓑ Ⓒ Ⓓ Ⓔ
46. [   ]
47. Ⓐ Ⓑ Ⓒ Ⓓ Ⓔ
48. Ⓐ Ⓑ Ⓒ Ⓓ Ⓔ
49. Ⓐ Ⓑ Ⓒ Ⓓ Ⓔ
50. Ⓐ Ⓑ Ⓒ Ⓓ Ⓔ
51. Ⓐ Ⓑ Ⓒ Ⓓ Ⓔ
52. [   ]
53. Ⓐ Ⓑ Ⓒ Ⓓ Ⓔ
54. Ⓐ Ⓑ Ⓒ Ⓓ Ⓔ
55. [   ]
56. Ⓐ Ⓑ Ⓒ Ⓓ Ⓔ
57. Ⓐ Ⓑ Ⓒ Ⓓ Ⓔ
58. Ⓐ Ⓑ Ⓒ Ⓓ Ⓔ
59. Ⓐ Ⓑ Ⓒ Ⓓ Ⓔ
60. Ⓐ Ⓑ Ⓒ Ⓓ Ⓔ
61. Ⓐ Ⓑ Ⓒ Ⓓ Ⓔ
62. Ⓐ Ⓑ Ⓒ Ⓓ Ⓔ
63. Ⓐ Ⓑ Ⓒ Ⓓ Ⓔ
64. Ⓐ Ⓑ Ⓒ Ⓓ Ⓔ
65. Ⓐ Ⓑ Ⓒ Ⓓ Ⓔ
66. Ⓐ Ⓑ Ⓒ Ⓓ Ⓔ
67. [   ]
68. Ⓐ Ⓑ Ⓒ Ⓓ Ⓔ
69. Ⓐ Ⓑ Ⓒ Ⓓ Ⓔ
70. Ⓐ Ⓑ Ⓒ Ⓓ Ⓔ

CLEP COLLEGE ALGEBRA
TEST 2

1. Ⓐ Ⓑ Ⓒ Ⓓ Ⓔ
2. Ⓐ Ⓑ Ⓒ Ⓓ Ⓔ
3. Ⓐ Ⓑ Ⓒ Ⓓ Ⓔ
4. Ⓐ Ⓑ Ⓒ Ⓓ Ⓔ
5. Ⓐ Ⓑ Ⓒ Ⓓ Ⓔ
6. Ⓐ Ⓑ Ⓒ Ⓓ Ⓔ
7. Ⓐ Ⓑ Ⓒ Ⓓ Ⓔ
8. Ⓐ Ⓑ Ⓒ Ⓓ Ⓔ
9. Ⓐ Ⓑ Ⓒ Ⓓ Ⓔ
10. Ⓐ Ⓑ Ⓒ Ⓓ Ⓔ
11. Ⓐ Ⓑ Ⓒ Ⓓ Ⓔ
12. Ⓐ Ⓑ Ⓒ Ⓓ Ⓔ
13. Ⓐ Ⓑ Ⓒ Ⓓ Ⓔ
14. Ⓐ Ⓑ Ⓒ Ⓓ Ⓔ
15. Ⓐ Ⓑ Ⓒ Ⓓ Ⓔ
16. Ⓐ Ⓑ Ⓒ Ⓓ Ⓔ
17. Ⓐ Ⓑ Ⓒ Ⓓ Ⓔ
18. Ⓐ Ⓑ Ⓒ Ⓓ Ⓔ
19. [_____]
20. Ⓐ Ⓑ Ⓒ Ⓓ Ⓔ
21. Ⓐ Ⓑ Ⓒ Ⓓ Ⓔ
22. Ⓐ Ⓑ Ⓒ Ⓓ Ⓔ
23. Ⓐ Ⓑ Ⓒ Ⓓ Ⓔ
24. Ⓐ Ⓑ Ⓒ Ⓓ Ⓔ
25. Ⓐ Ⓑ Ⓒ Ⓓ Ⓔ
26. Ⓐ Ⓑ Ⓒ Ⓓ Ⓔ
27. Ⓐ Ⓑ Ⓒ Ⓓ Ⓔ
28. Ⓐ Ⓑ Ⓒ Ⓓ Ⓔ
29. Ⓐ Ⓑ Ⓒ Ⓓ Ⓔ
30. Ⓐ Ⓑ Ⓒ Ⓓ Ⓔ
31. [_____]
32. Ⓐ Ⓑ Ⓒ Ⓓ Ⓔ
33. Ⓐ Ⓑ Ⓒ Ⓓ Ⓔ
34. [_____]
35. Ⓐ Ⓑ Ⓒ Ⓓ Ⓔ

36. Ⓐ Ⓑ Ⓒ Ⓓ Ⓔ
37. Ⓐ Ⓑ Ⓒ Ⓓ Ⓔ
38. Ⓐ Ⓑ Ⓒ Ⓓ Ⓔ
39. Ⓐ Ⓑ Ⓒ Ⓓ Ⓔ
40. [_____]
41. Ⓐ Ⓑ Ⓒ Ⓓ Ⓔ
42. Ⓐ Ⓑ Ⓒ Ⓓ Ⓔ
43. Ⓐ Ⓑ Ⓒ Ⓓ Ⓔ
44. Ⓐ Ⓑ Ⓒ Ⓓ Ⓔ
45. Ⓐ Ⓑ Ⓒ Ⓓ Ⓔ
46. Ⓐ Ⓑ Ⓒ Ⓓ Ⓔ
47. Ⓐ Ⓑ Ⓒ Ⓓ Ⓔ
48. [_____]
49. Ⓐ Ⓑ Ⓒ Ⓓ Ⓔ
50. Ⓐ Ⓑ Ⓒ Ⓓ Ⓔ
51. Ⓐ Ⓑ Ⓒ Ⓓ Ⓔ
52. Ⓐ Ⓑ Ⓒ Ⓓ Ⓔ
53. Ⓐ Ⓑ Ⓒ Ⓓ Ⓔ
54. Ⓐ Ⓑ Ⓒ Ⓓ Ⓔ
55. Ⓐ Ⓑ Ⓒ Ⓓ Ⓔ
56. Ⓐ Ⓑ Ⓒ Ⓓ Ⓔ
57. [_____]
58. [_____]
59. Ⓐ Ⓑ Ⓒ Ⓓ Ⓔ
60. Ⓐ Ⓑ Ⓒ Ⓓ Ⓔ
61. Ⓐ Ⓑ Ⓒ Ⓓ Ⓔ
62. Ⓐ Ⓑ Ⓒ Ⓓ Ⓔ
63. Ⓐ Ⓑ Ⓒ Ⓓ Ⓔ
64. [_____]
65. Ⓐ Ⓑ Ⓒ Ⓓ Ⓔ
66. Ⓐ Ⓑ Ⓒ Ⓓ Ⓔ
67. Ⓐ Ⓑ Ⓒ Ⓓ Ⓔ
68. Ⓐ Ⓑ Ⓒ Ⓓ Ⓔ
69. Ⓐ Ⓑ Ⓒ Ⓓ Ⓔ
70. Ⓐ Ⓑ Ⓒ Ⓓ Ⓔ

CLEP COLLEGE ALGEBRA
TEST 3

1. Ⓐ Ⓑ Ⓒ Ⓓ Ⓔ
2. [   ]
3. Ⓐ Ⓑ Ⓒ Ⓓ Ⓔ
4. Ⓐ Ⓑ Ⓒ Ⓓ Ⓔ
5. [   ]
6. Ⓐ Ⓑ Ⓒ Ⓓ Ⓔ
7. Ⓐ Ⓑ Ⓒ Ⓓ Ⓔ
8. Ⓐ Ⓑ Ⓒ Ⓓ Ⓔ
9. Ⓐ Ⓑ Ⓒ Ⓓ Ⓔ
10. [   ]
11. Ⓐ Ⓑ Ⓒ Ⓓ Ⓔ
12. Ⓐ Ⓑ Ⓒ Ⓓ Ⓔ
13. Ⓐ Ⓑ Ⓒ Ⓓ Ⓔ
14. Ⓐ Ⓑ Ⓒ Ⓓ Ⓔ
15. Ⓐ Ⓑ Ⓒ Ⓓ Ⓔ
16. Ⓐ Ⓑ Ⓒ Ⓓ Ⓔ
17. Ⓐ Ⓑ Ⓒ Ⓓ Ⓔ
18. Ⓐ Ⓑ Ⓒ Ⓓ Ⓔ
19. Ⓐ Ⓑ Ⓒ Ⓓ Ⓔ
20. Ⓐ Ⓑ Ⓒ Ⓓ Ⓔ
21. Ⓐ Ⓑ Ⓒ Ⓓ Ⓔ
22. Ⓐ Ⓑ Ⓒ Ⓓ Ⓔ
23. Ⓐ Ⓑ Ⓒ Ⓓ Ⓔ
24. Ⓐ Ⓑ Ⓒ Ⓓ Ⓔ
25. Ⓐ Ⓑ Ⓒ Ⓓ Ⓔ
26. Ⓐ Ⓑ Ⓒ Ⓓ Ⓔ
27. Ⓐ Ⓑ Ⓒ Ⓓ Ⓔ
28. Ⓐ Ⓑ Ⓒ Ⓓ Ⓔ
29. Ⓐ Ⓑ Ⓒ Ⓓ Ⓔ
30. Ⓐ Ⓑ Ⓒ Ⓓ Ⓔ
31. [   ]
32. Ⓐ Ⓑ Ⓒ Ⓓ Ⓔ
33. Ⓐ Ⓑ Ⓒ Ⓓ Ⓔ
34. Ⓐ Ⓑ Ⓒ Ⓓ Ⓔ
35. Ⓐ Ⓑ Ⓒ Ⓓ Ⓔ

36. Ⓐ Ⓑ Ⓒ Ⓓ Ⓔ
37. Ⓐ Ⓑ Ⓒ Ⓓ Ⓔ
38. Ⓐ Ⓑ Ⓒ Ⓓ Ⓔ
39. Ⓐ Ⓑ Ⓒ Ⓓ Ⓔ
40. Ⓐ Ⓑ Ⓒ Ⓓ Ⓔ
41. Ⓐ Ⓑ Ⓒ Ⓓ Ⓔ
42. Ⓐ Ⓑ Ⓒ Ⓓ Ⓔ
43. Ⓐ Ⓑ Ⓒ Ⓓ Ⓔ
44. Ⓐ Ⓑ Ⓒ Ⓓ Ⓔ
45. Ⓐ Ⓑ Ⓒ Ⓓ Ⓔ
46. Ⓐ Ⓑ Ⓒ Ⓓ Ⓔ
47. Ⓐ Ⓑ Ⓒ Ⓓ Ⓔ
48. Ⓐ Ⓑ Ⓒ Ⓓ Ⓔ
49. Ⓐ Ⓑ Ⓒ Ⓓ Ⓔ
50. Ⓐ Ⓑ Ⓒ Ⓓ Ⓔ
51. Ⓐ Ⓑ Ⓒ Ⓓ Ⓔ
52. Ⓐ Ⓑ Ⓒ Ⓓ Ⓔ
53. Ⓐ Ⓑ Ⓒ Ⓓ Ⓔ
54. Ⓐ Ⓑ Ⓒ Ⓓ Ⓔ
55. Ⓐ Ⓑ Ⓒ Ⓓ Ⓔ
56. Ⓐ Ⓑ Ⓒ Ⓓ Ⓔ
57. Ⓐ Ⓑ Ⓒ Ⓓ Ⓔ
58. Ⓐ Ⓑ Ⓒ Ⓓ Ⓔ
59. [   ]
60. Ⓐ Ⓑ Ⓒ Ⓓ Ⓔ
61. Ⓐ Ⓑ Ⓒ Ⓓ Ⓔ
62. [   ]
63. Ⓐ Ⓑ Ⓒ Ⓓ Ⓔ
64. Ⓐ Ⓑ Ⓒ Ⓓ Ⓔ
65. Ⓐ Ⓑ Ⓒ Ⓓ Ⓔ
66. [   ]
67. Ⓐ Ⓑ Ⓒ Ⓓ Ⓔ
68. Ⓐ Ⓑ Ⓒ Ⓓ Ⓔ
69. Ⓐ Ⓑ Ⓒ Ⓓ Ⓔ
70. [   ]

CLEP COLLEGE ALGEBRA
TEST 1

1. Ⓐ Ⓑ Ⓒ Ⓓ Ⓔ
2. Ⓐ Ⓑ Ⓒ Ⓓ Ⓔ
3. Ⓐ Ⓑ Ⓒ Ⓓ Ⓔ
4. Ⓐ Ⓑ Ⓒ Ⓓ Ⓔ
5. Ⓐ Ⓑ Ⓒ Ⓓ Ⓔ
6. Ⓐ Ⓑ Ⓒ Ⓓ Ⓔ
7. Ⓐ Ⓑ Ⓒ Ⓓ Ⓔ
8. Ⓐ Ⓑ Ⓒ Ⓓ Ⓔ
9. Ⓐ Ⓑ Ⓒ Ⓓ Ⓔ
10. Ⓐ Ⓑ Ⓒ Ⓓ Ⓔ
11. Ⓐ Ⓑ Ⓒ Ⓓ Ⓔ
12. Ⓐ Ⓑ Ⓒ Ⓓ Ⓔ
13. Ⓐ Ⓑ Ⓒ Ⓓ Ⓔ
14. [   ]
15. Ⓐ Ⓑ Ⓒ Ⓓ Ⓔ
16. Ⓐ Ⓑ Ⓒ Ⓓ Ⓔ
17. Ⓐ Ⓑ Ⓒ Ⓓ Ⓔ
18. Ⓐ Ⓑ Ⓒ Ⓓ Ⓔ
19. [   ]
20. Ⓐ Ⓑ Ⓒ Ⓓ Ⓔ
21. Ⓐ Ⓑ Ⓒ Ⓓ Ⓔ
22. Ⓐ Ⓑ Ⓒ Ⓓ Ⓔ
23. Ⓐ Ⓑ Ⓒ Ⓓ Ⓔ
24. Ⓐ Ⓑ Ⓒ Ⓓ Ⓔ
25. [   ]
26. Ⓐ Ⓑ Ⓒ Ⓓ Ⓔ
27. Ⓐ Ⓑ Ⓒ Ⓓ Ⓔ
28. Ⓐ Ⓑ Ⓒ Ⓓ Ⓔ
29. Ⓐ Ⓑ Ⓒ Ⓓ Ⓔ
30. Ⓐ Ⓑ Ⓒ Ⓓ Ⓔ
31. Ⓐ Ⓑ Ⓒ Ⓓ Ⓔ
32. Ⓐ Ⓑ Ⓒ Ⓓ Ⓔ
33. Ⓐ Ⓑ Ⓒ Ⓓ Ⓔ
34. Ⓐ Ⓑ Ⓒ Ⓓ Ⓔ
35. Ⓐ Ⓑ Ⓒ Ⓓ Ⓔ

36. Ⓐ Ⓑ Ⓒ Ⓓ Ⓔ
37. Ⓐ Ⓑ Ⓒ Ⓓ Ⓔ
38. [   ]
39. [   ]
40. Ⓐ Ⓑ Ⓒ Ⓓ Ⓔ
41. Ⓐ Ⓑ Ⓒ Ⓓ Ⓔ
42. Ⓐ Ⓑ Ⓒ Ⓓ Ⓔ
43. Ⓐ Ⓑ Ⓒ Ⓓ Ⓔ
44. Ⓐ Ⓑ Ⓒ Ⓓ Ⓔ
45. Ⓐ Ⓑ Ⓒ Ⓓ Ⓔ
46. [   ]
47. Ⓐ Ⓑ Ⓒ Ⓓ Ⓔ
48. Ⓐ Ⓑ Ⓒ Ⓓ Ⓔ
49. Ⓐ Ⓑ Ⓒ Ⓓ Ⓔ
50. Ⓐ Ⓑ Ⓒ Ⓓ Ⓔ
51. Ⓐ Ⓑ Ⓒ Ⓓ Ⓔ
52. [   ]
53. Ⓐ Ⓑ Ⓒ Ⓓ Ⓔ
54. Ⓐ Ⓑ Ⓒ Ⓓ Ⓔ
55. [   ]
56. Ⓐ Ⓑ Ⓒ Ⓓ Ⓔ
57. Ⓐ Ⓑ Ⓒ Ⓓ Ⓔ
58. Ⓐ Ⓑ Ⓒ Ⓓ Ⓔ
59. Ⓐ Ⓑ Ⓒ Ⓓ Ⓔ
60. Ⓐ Ⓑ Ⓒ Ⓓ Ⓔ
61. Ⓐ Ⓑ Ⓒ Ⓓ Ⓔ
62. Ⓐ Ⓑ Ⓒ Ⓓ Ⓔ
63. Ⓐ Ⓑ Ⓒ Ⓓ Ⓔ
64. Ⓐ Ⓑ Ⓒ Ⓓ Ⓔ
65. Ⓐ Ⓑ Ⓒ Ⓓ Ⓔ
66. Ⓐ Ⓑ Ⓒ Ⓓ Ⓔ
67. [   ]
68. Ⓐ Ⓑ Ⓒ Ⓓ Ⓔ
69. Ⓐ Ⓑ Ⓒ Ⓓ Ⓔ
70. Ⓐ Ⓑ Ⓒ Ⓓ Ⓔ

CLEP COLLEGE ALGEBRA
TEST 2

1. Ⓐ Ⓑ Ⓒ Ⓓ Ⓔ
2. Ⓐ Ⓑ Ⓒ Ⓓ Ⓔ
3. Ⓐ Ⓑ Ⓒ Ⓓ Ⓔ
4. Ⓐ Ⓑ Ⓒ Ⓓ Ⓔ
5. Ⓐ Ⓑ Ⓒ Ⓓ Ⓔ
6. Ⓐ Ⓑ Ⓒ Ⓓ Ⓔ
7. Ⓐ Ⓑ Ⓒ Ⓓ Ⓔ
8. Ⓐ Ⓑ Ⓒ Ⓓ Ⓔ
9. Ⓐ Ⓑ Ⓒ Ⓓ Ⓔ
10. Ⓐ Ⓑ Ⓒ Ⓓ Ⓔ
11. Ⓐ Ⓑ Ⓒ Ⓓ Ⓔ
12. Ⓐ Ⓑ Ⓒ Ⓓ Ⓔ
13. Ⓐ Ⓑ Ⓒ Ⓓ Ⓔ
14. Ⓐ Ⓑ Ⓒ Ⓓ Ⓔ
15. Ⓐ Ⓑ Ⓒ Ⓓ Ⓔ
16. Ⓐ Ⓑ Ⓒ Ⓓ Ⓔ
17. Ⓐ Ⓑ Ⓒ Ⓓ Ⓔ
18. Ⓐ Ⓑ Ⓒ Ⓓ Ⓔ
19. [   ]
20. Ⓐ Ⓑ Ⓒ Ⓓ Ⓔ
21. Ⓐ Ⓑ Ⓒ Ⓓ Ⓔ
22. Ⓐ Ⓑ Ⓒ Ⓓ Ⓔ
23. Ⓐ Ⓑ Ⓒ Ⓓ Ⓔ
24. Ⓐ Ⓑ Ⓒ Ⓓ Ⓔ
25. Ⓐ Ⓑ Ⓒ Ⓓ Ⓔ
26. Ⓐ Ⓑ Ⓒ Ⓓ Ⓔ
27. Ⓐ Ⓑ Ⓒ Ⓓ Ⓔ
28. Ⓐ Ⓑ Ⓒ Ⓓ Ⓔ
29. Ⓐ Ⓑ Ⓒ Ⓓ Ⓔ
30. Ⓐ Ⓑ Ⓒ Ⓓ Ⓔ
31. [   ]
32. Ⓐ Ⓑ Ⓒ Ⓓ Ⓔ
33. Ⓐ Ⓑ Ⓒ Ⓓ Ⓔ
34. [   ]
35. Ⓐ Ⓑ Ⓒ Ⓓ Ⓔ

36. Ⓐ Ⓑ Ⓒ Ⓓ Ⓔ
37. Ⓐ Ⓑ Ⓒ Ⓓ Ⓔ
38. Ⓐ Ⓑ Ⓒ Ⓓ Ⓔ
39. Ⓐ Ⓑ Ⓒ Ⓓ Ⓔ
40. [   ]
41. Ⓐ Ⓑ Ⓒ Ⓓ Ⓔ
42. Ⓐ Ⓑ Ⓒ Ⓓ Ⓔ
43. Ⓐ Ⓑ Ⓒ Ⓓ Ⓔ
44. Ⓐ Ⓑ Ⓒ Ⓓ Ⓔ
45. Ⓐ Ⓑ Ⓒ Ⓓ Ⓔ
46. Ⓐ Ⓑ Ⓒ Ⓓ Ⓔ
47. Ⓐ Ⓑ Ⓒ Ⓓ Ⓔ
48. [   ]
49. Ⓐ Ⓑ Ⓒ Ⓓ Ⓔ
50. Ⓐ Ⓑ Ⓒ Ⓓ Ⓔ
51. Ⓐ Ⓑ Ⓒ Ⓓ Ⓔ
52. Ⓐ Ⓑ Ⓒ Ⓓ Ⓔ
53. Ⓐ Ⓑ Ⓒ Ⓓ Ⓔ
54. Ⓐ Ⓑ Ⓒ Ⓓ Ⓔ
55. Ⓐ Ⓑ Ⓒ Ⓓ Ⓔ
56. Ⓐ Ⓑ Ⓒ Ⓓ Ⓔ
57. [   ]
58. [   ]
59. Ⓐ Ⓑ Ⓒ Ⓓ Ⓔ
60. Ⓐ Ⓑ Ⓒ Ⓓ Ⓔ
61. Ⓐ Ⓑ Ⓒ Ⓓ Ⓔ
62. Ⓐ Ⓑ Ⓒ Ⓓ Ⓔ
63. Ⓐ Ⓑ Ⓒ Ⓓ Ⓔ
64. [   ]
65. Ⓐ Ⓑ Ⓒ Ⓓ Ⓔ
66. Ⓐ Ⓑ Ⓒ Ⓓ Ⓔ
67. Ⓐ Ⓑ Ⓒ Ⓓ Ⓔ
68. Ⓐ Ⓑ Ⓒ Ⓓ Ⓔ
69. Ⓐ Ⓑ Ⓒ Ⓓ Ⓔ
70. Ⓐ Ⓑ Ⓒ Ⓓ Ⓔ

CLEP COLLEGE ALGEBRA
TEST 3

1. Ⓐ Ⓑ Ⓒ Ⓓ Ⓔ
2. [   ]
3. Ⓐ Ⓑ Ⓒ Ⓓ Ⓔ
4. Ⓐ Ⓑ Ⓒ Ⓓ Ⓔ
5. [   ]
6. Ⓐ Ⓑ Ⓒ Ⓓ Ⓔ
7. Ⓐ Ⓑ Ⓒ Ⓓ Ⓔ
8. Ⓐ Ⓑ Ⓒ Ⓓ Ⓔ
9. Ⓐ Ⓑ Ⓒ Ⓓ Ⓔ
10. [   ]
11. Ⓐ Ⓑ Ⓒ Ⓓ Ⓔ
12. Ⓐ Ⓑ Ⓒ Ⓓ Ⓔ
13. Ⓐ Ⓑ Ⓒ Ⓓ Ⓔ
14. Ⓐ Ⓑ Ⓒ Ⓓ Ⓔ
15. Ⓐ Ⓑ Ⓒ Ⓓ Ⓔ
16. Ⓐ Ⓑ Ⓒ Ⓓ Ⓔ
17. Ⓐ Ⓑ Ⓒ Ⓓ Ⓔ
18. Ⓐ Ⓑ Ⓒ Ⓓ Ⓔ
19. Ⓐ Ⓑ Ⓒ Ⓓ Ⓔ
20. Ⓐ Ⓑ Ⓒ Ⓓ Ⓔ
21. Ⓐ Ⓑ Ⓒ Ⓓ Ⓔ
22. Ⓐ Ⓑ Ⓒ Ⓓ Ⓔ
23. Ⓐ Ⓑ Ⓒ Ⓓ Ⓔ
24. Ⓐ Ⓑ Ⓒ Ⓓ Ⓔ
25. Ⓐ Ⓑ Ⓒ Ⓓ Ⓔ
26. Ⓐ Ⓑ Ⓒ Ⓓ Ⓔ
27. Ⓐ Ⓑ Ⓒ Ⓓ Ⓔ
28. Ⓐ Ⓑ Ⓒ Ⓓ Ⓔ
29. Ⓐ Ⓑ Ⓒ Ⓓ Ⓔ
30. Ⓐ Ⓑ Ⓒ Ⓓ Ⓔ
31. [   ]
32. Ⓐ Ⓑ Ⓒ Ⓓ Ⓔ
33. Ⓐ Ⓑ Ⓒ Ⓓ Ⓔ
34. Ⓐ Ⓑ Ⓒ Ⓓ Ⓔ
35. Ⓐ Ⓑ Ⓒ Ⓓ Ⓔ

36. Ⓐ Ⓑ Ⓒ Ⓓ Ⓔ
37. Ⓐ Ⓑ Ⓒ Ⓓ Ⓔ
38. Ⓐ Ⓑ Ⓒ Ⓓ Ⓔ
39. Ⓐ Ⓑ Ⓒ Ⓓ Ⓔ
40. Ⓐ Ⓑ Ⓒ Ⓓ Ⓔ
41. Ⓐ Ⓑ Ⓒ Ⓓ Ⓔ
42. Ⓐ Ⓑ Ⓒ Ⓓ Ⓔ
43. Ⓐ Ⓑ Ⓒ Ⓓ Ⓔ
44. Ⓐ Ⓑ Ⓒ Ⓓ Ⓔ
45. Ⓐ Ⓑ Ⓒ Ⓓ Ⓔ
46. Ⓐ Ⓑ Ⓒ Ⓓ Ⓔ
47. Ⓐ Ⓑ Ⓒ Ⓓ Ⓔ
48. Ⓐ Ⓑ Ⓒ Ⓓ Ⓔ
49. Ⓐ Ⓑ Ⓒ Ⓓ Ⓔ
50. Ⓐ Ⓑ Ⓒ Ⓓ Ⓔ
51. Ⓐ Ⓑ Ⓒ Ⓓ Ⓔ
52. Ⓐ Ⓑ Ⓒ Ⓓ Ⓔ
53. Ⓐ Ⓑ Ⓒ Ⓓ Ⓔ
54. Ⓐ Ⓑ Ⓒ Ⓓ Ⓔ
55. Ⓐ Ⓑ Ⓒ Ⓓ Ⓔ
56. Ⓐ Ⓑ Ⓒ Ⓓ Ⓔ
57. Ⓐ Ⓑ Ⓒ Ⓓ Ⓔ
58. Ⓐ Ⓑ Ⓒ Ⓓ Ⓔ
59. [   ]
60. Ⓐ Ⓑ Ⓒ Ⓓ Ⓔ
61. Ⓐ Ⓑ Ⓒ Ⓓ Ⓔ
62. [   ]
63. Ⓐ Ⓑ Ⓒ Ⓓ Ⓔ
64. Ⓐ Ⓑ Ⓒ Ⓓ Ⓔ
65. Ⓐ Ⓑ Ⓒ Ⓓ Ⓔ
66. [   ]
67. Ⓐ Ⓑ Ⓒ Ⓓ Ⓔ
68. Ⓐ Ⓑ Ⓒ Ⓓ Ⓔ
69. Ⓐ Ⓑ Ⓒ Ⓓ Ⓔ
70. [   ]

REA's Test Prep Books Are The Best!

(a sample of the <u>hundreds of letters</u> REA receives each year)

(more on front page)